WITHDRAWN
NDSU

CASS LIBRARY OF AFRICAN STUDIES

AFRICAN PREHISTORY
No. 3

General Editor: Professor BRIAN FAGAN
Department of Anthropology, University of California, Santa Barbara

MEDIAEVAL RHODESIA

AFRICAN PREHISTORY

No. 1. Gertrude Caton Thompson
The Zimbabwe Culture. Ruins and reactions (1931).
With a new introduction by the author.
Second Edition

No. 2. L. S. B. Leakey
The Stone Age Cultures of Kenya Colony (1931).
With a new introductory note by the author.
New Impression

No. 3. David Randall-MacIver
Mediaeval Rhodesia (1906).
With an introductory note by Brian Fagan.
New Impression

No. 4. James Theodore Bent
The Ruined Cities of Mashonaland: being a record of excavation and exploration in 1891 (1892; 3rd ed. 1895).
New Impression

No. 5. Richard Nicklin Hall
Great Zimbabwe, Mashonaland, Rhodesia: an account of two years examination work in 1902–4 on behalf of the Government of Rhodesia (1905).
New Impression

No. 6. Edward Humphrey Lane Poole
The Native Tribes of the Eastern Province of Northern Rhodesia. Notes on their migrations and history (2nd ed. 1938).
New Impression

No. 7. Miles Crawford Burkitt
South Africa's Past in Stone and Paint (1928). With a new preface by the author.
New Impression

No. 8. Astley John Hilary Goodwin and Clarence Van Riet Lowe
The Stone Age Cultures of South Africa (1929).
New Impression

No. 9. Louis Péringuey
The Stone Ages of South Africa as represented in the collection of the South African Museum (1911).
New Impression

No. 10. Anthony John Arkell
Shaheinab. An account of the excavation of a Neolithic occupation site carried out for the Sudan Antiquities Service in 1949–50 (1953).
New Impression

FRONTISPIECE

(*a*) NANATALI, FRONT. *See pages* 51-55.

(*b*) NANATALI, FRONT. *See pages* 51-55.

Mediaeval Rhodesia

by

David Randall-MacIver

With a new introductory note by

Professor Brian Fagan

Department of Anthropology, University of California, Santa Barbara

FRANK CASS & CO. LTD.

1971

Published by
FRANK CASS AND COMPANY LIMITED
67 Great Russell Street, London WC1B 3BT

Introductory note Copyright © 1971 Brian Fagan

All rights reserved

First edition 1906
New impression with
a new introductory note 1971

ISBN 0 7146 1885 3

Printed in Great Britain by Clarke, Doble & Brendon Ltd.
Plymouth and London

TO

SIR LEWIS MICHELL

WHOSE INTEREST IN ARCHÆOLOGY

ORIGINATED THE RESEARCHES THEREIN DESCRIBED

THIS VOLUME IS DEDICATED

INTRODUCTORY NOTE

The monograph which is reprinted here was an important landmark in the investigation of the Zimbabwe Ruins. In the early years of this century, it was the custom of the British Association for the Advancement of Science to hold regular meetings in various countries of the British Empire, in order to encourage scientific research in other parts of the world. The Association planned a meeting in South Africa in 1905 and commissioned a young archaeologist from England, Dr. David Randall-MacIver, to carry out excavations at Zimbabwe and to report on the significance of this remarkable monument.

Randall-MacIver was the first professional archaeologist to examine the Ruins and was well qualified to do so. Although he had no African experience he was trained by the eminent Egyptologist, Sir Flinders Petrie, a pioneer in sequence dating and typographical analysis. MacIver's methods were vastly different from those of Bent and Hall and others who had preceeded him. He investigated other ruins as well as Zimbabwe, and took careful note of the minor domestic finds made in his trenches, in contrast to earlier investigators who tend to concentrate on more flamboyant artifacts and exotic objects. He made comparisons between the pottery of Zimbabwe and that of the people living in the area in 1905. His careful use of African artifacts and of comparisons with modern material culture, led him to believe that the people who inhabited Zimbabwe were related to the inhabitants of the area in the early 20th century. As Summers points out, his approach was in direct contrast to that of his antiquarian predecessors for he used *all* the objects found at the site as evidence, and not just a selected few. He had no preconceived ideas, and used new methods of dating to establish a relative chronology of the various periods of occupation of the Rhodesian ruins, by careful study of the imported porcelain and china found at Zimbabwe. British Museum experts were able to assign the imported vessel to the 13th century A.D. and later.

In contrast to Hall, MacIver firmly stated that Zimbabwe was of African origin and inspiration and belonged to the Mediaeval period, the date being established by foreign imports the age of which could be established with some exactitude. The publication of *Mediaeval Rhodesia* caused a furious academic controversy, led by Richard Hall, who until that time had been regarded as the world authority on Rhodesia in general and on Zimbabwe in particular. Those who assigned a high antiquity to Zimbabwe were bitterly angry. The echoes of this controversy still linger on, but the basic reliability of Randall-MacIver's work was recognized by many serious scientists of the time. His results were broadly confirmed in 1929, when Gertrude Caton Thompson carried out further work at Zimbabwe, again under the auspices of the British Association. But MacIver's early work set the stage for the recognition of Zimbabwe as one of the greatest achievements of prehistoric Africa.

The reader is referred to Roger Summers' *Zimbabwe: A Rhodesian Mystery* (Johannesburg, 1963) for further information.

University of California
1970

Brian Fagan

PREFACE

The investigations which are described in this volume were undertaken during the spring and summer of 1905 at the invitation and with the support of the British Association and the Rhodes Trustees. Though the problems of the origin and date of the ruins in Rhodesia had been before the public for a whole generation, from the time, in fact, that Mauch rediscovered Zimbabwe, yet remarkably little progress had been made towards their solution. In part this was due to the difficulty of exploring a country that has only recently been opened up, in part to the concentration of attention upon one single group out of all the numerous ruins which were available for study, and in part to the want of system with which any excavations had been conducted.

The British Association, when arranging to visit South Africa in 1905, resolved to make an effort to end this uncertainty, and asked me to precede the visitors by some months in order to explore and to prepare a special report upon the subject of the ruins. I reached Southern Rhodesia early in April and continued at work till the middle of September. Owing to the great improvements effected in the means of communication and to the exceptional facilities accorded me, I was enabled to conduct researches over a great extent of country, and to obtain observations which have led to unexpectedly definite conclusions.

These conclusions are not of the nature which the general public expected, though archæologists and ethnologists see no reason to be surprised at them. Before there was sufficient evidence on which to base any suggestions whatsoever as to origin or date, popular opinion had confidently settled the question to its own great satisfaction. It had decided that the Rhodesian ruins must be of immense antiquity, and, following the mediæval chroniclers with an uncritical credulity that would have been as admirable in their days as it is unworthy in our own, had pronounced Zimbabwe and all similar buildings to be the work of an ancient people from the East. Journalists and popular writers professed, as might be expected, a knowledge of lost ancient history which the most learned Orientalists do not dream of claiming.

Still it was possible, of course, that these romanticists might prove to be correct; although only guessing, they might have blundered on the truth. Certainly even in the spring of 1905 it could be asserted positively that nothing had then been obtained from the ruins which an archæologist could recognise as more than a few centuries old; and that the objects, when not immediately recognisable as mediæval imports, were of characteristically African type. But the excavations which had been conducted by various untrained amateurs left still undecided the question whether older strata did not exist beneath the mass of what was unquestionably mediæval and native African. It was this that I had to determine; and that I approached the problem without bias will readily be believed by those who are aware that for the past nine years my chief interest has been in the archæology of Egypt and the East. Nothing therefore could have been more attractive to me than the prospect of extending the range of Oriental studies to South-East Africa; and if it has been necessary to abandon that dream, it is because it has proved to be incompatible with any respect for science and the logic of observed facts.

Yet if my new view as to the origin of the Rhodesian ruins and their builders dissipates the false halo which has been cast about them, it confers advantages which more than compensate for the loss. As a consequence of it the monuments are brought into direct association with the country in which they are found, and there is opened up a new field of research which should fascinate the imagination and stir the energies of Rhodesians. The problems of the past are shown to be linked with those of the present; student and settler may unite in the patriotic task of solving them.

My report, being wholly independent and original, may be judged upon its own merits, and it will be sufficiently clear why little or no reference has been made to various books which it was impossible to praise and would have been invidious to criticise. A single honourable exception must be made. There is one work of sterling scholarship which ought to be familiar to all who profess an interest in these subjects, namely, Dr. G. M. Theal's *Records of South-Eastern Africa*. It will frequently be quoted in the following pages under the abbreviation *T.R.*, with the accompanying number of volume and page. Apart from the collection of documents embodied in that admirable work, there exists no bibliography with which the student need be troubled.

PREFACE

This Preface cannot be concluded without acknowledgment, however brief, of many debts of gratitude. To the generous support of the Rhodes Trustees my expedition owes its origin, and to the assistance received from their representatives in South Africa much of any success that it may have achieved. The unfailing kindness of administrators, magistrates, and settlers in every part of the country has been appreciated more deeply than can be expressed within such narrow limits; and should these lines meet the eye of any out of all those who have been my friends upon the veldt, they will, I hope, accept them as some slight record of my thanks.

In the preparation of the volume, apart from obligations which are specially mentioned in the text, I have been aided by Mr. N. W. Thomas, who revised my proofs; by Mr. Ellis Allen of Bulawayo, who drew the pottery and copied my plans for publication; and by Messrs. Smart & Copley of Bulawayo, who skilfully developed a large number of my negatives. The photographs were, without exception, taken by myself, the scale on which ornaments and implements are represented being approximately one-fourth. Of the plans, three (those of Dhlo-Dhlo, Nanatali, and Zimbabwe) are not my own, but are reproduced by kind permission of the Scientific Association of Bulawayo.

The name of my esteemed colleague Mr. E. M. Andrews has been reserved for a special word at the close. From the day when our common interest in archæology made us friends at Umtali, Mr. Andrews was always my loyal and indefatigable associate. He worked on alone at Umtali while I was away in Inyanga, and obtained a brilliant success which was the just reward of several years of patient exploration. We were together after that time upon all the sites which are hereafter to be described. If he is able to carry out his projected exploration of the ruins in Portuguese territory, Mr. Andrews will have contributed largely to the progress of South African archæology.

D. R.-M.

CONTENTS

CHAPTER I
INTRODUCTORY—INYANGA . . . . PAGE 1

CHAPTER II
THE NIEKERK RUINS 14

CHAPTER III
THE NIEKERK RUINS (*continued*)—THE PLACE OF OFFERINGS . . 30

CHAPTER IV
UMTALI 35

CHAPTER V
DHLO-DHLO 38

CHAPTER VI
NANATALI AND KHAMI 51

CHAPTER VII
ZIMBABWE—DATING OF THE "ELLIPTICAL TEMPLE" . . . 59

CHAPTER VIII
ZIMBABWE—DESCRIPTION OF THE "ELLIPTICAL TEMPLE" . . 67

CHAPTER IX
ZIMBABWE. THE VALLEY RUINS. THE ACROPOLIS. OBJECTS FOUND . 75

CHAPTER X

Conclusion 83

APPENDIX I

Details of Trial-Sections in the "Elliptical Temple," Zimbabwe . 88

APPENDIX II

Notes 90

LIST OF PLATES

PLATE		
	Two Views of Front of Nanatali	*Frontispiece*
1.	Entrances of the Northern Fort, Inyanga	*between pages* 12-13
	Main Wall of the Eastern Fort, Inyanga, from inside	,,
2.	Plan of Eastern Fort at Inyanga	,,
	Main Wall of Eastern Fort, Inyanga, viewed from outside	,,
3.	Ground Plan of Pit-Dwelling at Inyanga	,,
	Top Surface of part of a Pit-Dwelling, Inyanga	,,
4.	Lighting-Hole of the Corridor of a Pit-Dwelling, Inyanga	,,
	Doorway of the Corridor of a Pit-Dwelling, Inyanga	,,
	Sections of the Corridor of Pit-Dwellings, Inyanga	,,
5.	Part of a Pit-Dwelling, Inyanga	,,
	Door and Corridor of a Pit-Dwelling, Inyanga	,,
6.	Two Views of the Niekerk Ruins	*between pages* 34-35
7.	A Place of Offerings, Niekerk Ruins	,,
	View of Niekerk Ruins	,,
8.	Two Plans of Buildings on the Niekerk Ruins	,,
9.	Six Plans of Buildings on the Niekerk Ruins	,,
10.	Pottery from the Niekerk Ruins	,,
11.	Pottery from the Niekerk Ruins	,,
12.	Iron Objects from Inyanga and the Niekerk Ruins	,,
	Objects from the Offering-place on the Niekerk Ruins	,,
	Stone Implements from the Niekerk Ruins	,,
	Stone Implements from the Débris Heap at Dhlo-Dhlo	,,
	Stone Implements from the Charter District	,,
13.	Diagrams of Two Forts on the Niekerk Ruins	,,
	Plan showing the Construction of the Altar at Umtali	,,

PLATE

14. Soapstone Carvings from Umtali . . . . . . *between pages* 38-39

　　Iron Objects from Umtali . . . . ”

　　"Fuba" Board on a Boulder, Umtali . . . . . ”

15. Soapstone Carvings from Umtali . . . . . . ”

16. Patterns of Pottery found at Umtali . . . . . ”

17. View of Front of Dhlo-Dhlo . . . . . . *between pages* 50-51

　　Sketch Plan of Central Part of Dhlo-Dhlo . . . . ”

18. Decoration on East Side of Main Entrance, Dhlo-Dhlo . . ”

　　Decoration on West Side of Main Entrance, Dhlo-Dhlo . . ”

19. Objects found with Nankin China beneath Floor of Hut in Citadel, Dhlo-Dhlo . . . . ”

20. Objects found in the Débris Heap at Dhlo-Dhlo . . . ”

21. Front of Nanatali, showing the Chief's Hut inside . . . *between pages* 58-59

　　Decorated Façade of Nanatali . . . . . . ”

22. Plan of Nanatali . . . . ”

23. East Ruin, Khami . . . . ”

　　Precipice Ruin, Khami . . . . ”

24. Two Huts outside the Precipice Ruin, Khami . . . . ”

25. Plan of the "Elliptical Temple," Zimbabwe . . . . *between pages* 74-75

26. Façade of the "Elliptical Temple," Zimbabwe . . . . ”

　　Interior of the "Elliptical Temple," Zimbabwe . . . ”

27. Section of Enclosure XV. in the "Elliptical Temple," Zimbabwe . ”

　　Photograph of the same Section . . . . . . ”

28. General View of the Valley Ruins, Zimbabwe . . . . *between pages* 82-83

　　View of the Philips Ruins in the Valley, Zimbabwe . . . ”

29. General View of the Acropolis, Zimbabwe . . . . ”

　　Part of the Western Temple on the Acropolis, Zimbabwe . ”

30. China and Beads of Ivory and Shell from Dhlo-Dhlo . . ”

　　Oriental Faience from Zimbabwe . . . . . ”

　　Gold, Copper, Bronze, and Enamelled Bronze from Zimbabwe . ”

31. Iron Weapons from Zimbabwe . . . . . . ”

32. Bone Amulets from Khami . . . . ”

　　Iron, Copper, and Bronze Articles from Khami . . . ”

LIST OF ILLUSTRATIONS

PLATE
33. Pottery from Dhlo-Dhlo . . . . *after page* 104
34. Pottery from Dhlo-Dhlo . . . . ,,
    Pottery from Khami . . . . ,,
35. Pottery from Khami . . . . ,,
    Pottery from Zimbabwe . . . . ,,
36. Stream and Irrigation Furrow, Inyanga . . . . . ,,
    Modern Hut and Grain-Shelter near Zimbabwe . . . . ,,

CHAPTER I

INTRODUCTORY—INYANGA

THE most appropriate entrance into Southern Rhodesia is from the east coast of Africa, for the commercial development of the country has always been mainly dependent upon the roads leading into it from the ports between Mozambique and Sofala. Its history is therefore inextricably interwoven with that of the foreign settlements, whether Arab or Portuguese, which form a chain from Lourenço Marques almost to the Gulf of Aden.

The east coast of Africa.

But here at the very outset let me utter a note of warning. There is no historical warrant for ascribing any high antiquity to any one of these east-coast colonies. Magadoxo, the earliest and the nearest of any importance to its parent Arabia, is known, from the chronicle which the Portuguese conquerors found at Kilwa, to have been founded not earlier than the middle of the tenth century A.D. Kilwa itself, a Persian settlement, is seventy years younger. And whatever the probabilities that Arab traders established themselves in very early days on both sides of the Red Sea and the Gulf of Aden, there is good reason to suppose that they seldom adventured much farther south until at least the later days of the Roman Empire. For the misconceptions of so learned a geographer as Ptolemy suggest that even in the second century after Christ the coast south of Cape Guardafui was still very imperfectly known.

From the second century to the tenth, when some little documentary evidence becomes available with the first Arab geographers and the far more valuable chronicle of Kilwa, is a dark period, on which but little light is thrown by a solitary work of unknown authorship and date, the famous Periplus of the Red Sea. If, however, we may trust M. Guillain's identifications of sites mentioned in the Periplus, we are led to the conclusion that at any rate some centuries before Mohammed an Arab Colony, Rhapta, had been

The east coast of Africa. planted as far south as the Rufiji, eight degrees beyond the equator. But this in itself suggests that the Zambesi was still unknown, since the author, who evidently derived his information from Arab sources, regarded Rhapta as his *ultima Thule*.[1]

The spade of some fortunate explorer may, in the future, bring to light traces of settlements on the east coast belonging to the centuries just before and after the beginning of the Mohammedan era, but we have no right to assume their existence until they are found. Unaided documentary evidence does not permit us to suppose that there was any Oriental traffic even with Sofala, the gate of the gold-bearing regions of the interior, prior to its establishment as a mart by the inhabitants of Magadoxo.

From Sofala westwards to the capital city of the Monomotapa was a journey of some three weeks for Duarte Barbosa and his contemporaries of the sixteenth century. The modern traveller may reach the Great Zimbabwe, which is generally identified with the place referred to, in a considerably shorter time, though by a more circuitous route. But he may be counselled not to hasten too much on the way; for there is much to interest the archæologist in the more outlying regions of that shadowy, but by no means mythical, dominion which the Portuguese writers describe with some exaggeration as an empire covering a great part of South-East Africa. The itinerary traced in these pages will lead the reader to sites which are not less interesting, even if they are less famous, than others which have often been described.

Umtali. The dangers which once beset the first stages of the journey from the coast have disappeared now that a train takes but a few hours to traverse the fever-stricken low veldt; and the most bigoted of æsthetes may bless the railway when he finds himself, only a day after quitting Beira, in the healthy and beautiful mountains of Umtali. Situated over 3000 feet above the sea, in an amphitheatre surrounded by granite and diorite hills, Umtali reminds the new-comer from Britain of highland regions in his own home. It is the first town seen after crossing the Portuguese border; and, as this volume does not deal with the numerous and important ruins along the line of the Revue, the Busi, or the Sabi rivers, it is the first halt to be recorded in this tour of exploration. We may well spend a few days here in a preliminary visit to a site which will be described in fuller detail in a later chapter. A walk of three miles south from the lower end of the town leads out to a series of kopjes

INTRODUCTORY—INYANGA

and tree-clad slopes trending upward to the higher hills which bound the horizon. Dense though the grass and undergrowth may be, rude walls of unhewn stone arrest the attention directly the path leaves the level ground. Examined more closely, they reveal more system than at first appears. Only a foot or two in height, they are built without mortar, and form circles, arcs of circles, or ellipses. It is difficult to distinguish ground-plans while the grass still stands shoulder-high, but when fires have bared the hillside in the winter months, the lines of stones may be traced and the design of the builders understood. Then it is seen that these constructions are isolated units, each complete in itself and independent of its neighbours. Either they are single rings or they are enclosures containing several rings surrounded by roughly-circular girdle-walls. Fresh from Europe and the Mediterranean, the sanguine archæologist will almost inevitably be reminded of the rude stone structures of Britain and France, North Africa, and Palestine; and may suppose that on the very first day of his explorations he has stumbled upon the goal of his ambitions, an ancient cemetery. But a little trial excavation brings disillusionment. These are not graves, nor is the secret of their purpose to be discovered in a day. It is only when other sites in different places have been studied that the Umtali ruins can be appreciated. So let us leave Umtali, to revisit it later when more experience has been gained, and travel in the direction of the Zambesi as far as Inyanga.

Umtali.

It is only about sixty miles due north from Umtali to Inyanga, but the direct track is exceptionally rough and difficult, so that it is preferable to take the train as far as Rusapi, a journey of four hours, and to proceed thence for fifty-five miles on horseback or by wagon. The road from Rusapi climbs continually upwards, affording magnificent views of characteristic Rhodesian scenery. Now and again a Kaffir kraal is seen, then there will be a wide expanse of level veldt, studded with abrupt kopjes in the foreground and middle distance; behind these, again, lofty mountains, whose grandeur is impaired only by their roundness of contour and the absence of peaks or crags.

Inyanga.

The homestead of Inyanga is in the middle of a fine estate of 100,000 acres, a favourite property of the late Mr. Cecil Rhodes and, now administered by his Trustees. Stock-raising, agriculture, and fruit-growing are the occupations of the hospitable managers of the farm, who yet found time to assist their guest in a thousand ways and to guide him to the chief points of interest in the neighbourhood. Standing no less than 6000 feet above the level of the

MEDIÆVAL RHODESIA

Inyanga. sea, the farm is surrounded by grassy uplands, and there is pasture for sheep even on the higher ridges that during the winter are constantly wrapped in mist, through which the great Inyanga mountain (9000 feet) is scarcely visible. The whole countryside teems with the monuments of bygone ages, to a description of which the remainder of this chapter will be devoted. The antiquities of Inyanga were described to the writer before his arrival as consisting of hill-forts, slave-pits, water-furrows, and terraces for cultivation. They may here be treated in that order.

Hill-forts. There are four ancient forts on the estate, so situated that one might fancy they had been built for the express purpose of defending the Rhodes farm. Each is, roughly, three miles distant from it, and it would be easy to signal across the intervening space. The photographs in Plates I. and II. will give an idea of their character and construction; Plate I. *a* shows part of the exterior of the Northern Fort with its entrances; Plate I. *b*, the main wall of the Eastern Fort as seen from the inside, and Plate II. *b*, another part of the same wall, from the outside.

The small Southern Fort stands in a commanding position at the top of a rather steep kopje, and is very roughly and carelessly constructed of large and small pieces of unworked granite, piled one upon the other, without mortar. In outline it is elliptical, and measures in greatest interior diameter 17×15 metres; there are no divisions or cross-walls of any kind inside. Where the wall is still standing, its average height is 2 metres, but it was never strongly built, and is ruined at several points. Its average width at the ground-level is 2 metres, or rather less, but half of this must be assigned to the rough banquette which runs round on the inside, a little below the top of the outer half of the wall. In several places there are loopholes; and there are three entrances, viz. on the North, North-west, and West, the character of which may be appreciated from the photographs in Plate I., where precisely similar entrances occurring in other forts are figured. These are simple gaps in the wall, just over 1 metre in height and 0.50 m. or 0.60 m. in width, roofed with large, flat, unhewn slabs of about 0.20 m. thickness. The Southern Fort is the most carelessly built and tumble-down construction in the whole of the Inyanga district; the fitting of the stones is very bad, and it is difficult to suppose that such a building, which could almost have been run up in a few hours, ever served as anything better than a mere temporary refuge in time of great need.

INYANGA

The Northern and North-Eastern Forts are similar in general character, and not very greatly superior in construction, but exhibit one or two features not found in the Southern. Thus, in the Northern Fort, though the walls and entrances are of the same kind, there are no loopholes; while, on the other hand, though there are no actual subdivisions in the interior, yet there are two small circles (2.50 m. in interior diameter) built up of two courses of boulders to a height of about 0.50 m. One of these is in the middle, and the other, abutting on it, is built against the inside of the southern wall. The fort is elliptical in outline, measuring 24 metres in maximum interior diameter; its wall is about 2 metres in height, and very variable in thickness. The kopje on which it is built is extremely steep, and intrenched with low lines of boulders from the bottom upwards.

The North-Eastern Fort, which stands in a most formidable position on a sheer cliff above the little Inyanga river, is, perhaps for that very reason, the most irregularly built of the four. In all the forts the outline of the wall is unsymmetrical, and adapts itself to every irregularity of the hillside, but in this case the plan is so formless that it can only be described as vacillating between an ellipse, a horse-shoe, and a rectangle, but approaching most nearly to the horse-shoe. Its maximum interior diameter is about 30 metres. The wall, which is not loopholed, stands in places as much as 2 metres high, averages 1.50 m. in thickness, and, as in the other cases, has a banquette on the inside. It is pierced with entrances of the usual kind, three in number. Inside there are no less than six of the low rings of stones noted as occurring in the Northern Fort; one of them being in the centre, the others against the east, south, and west walls. They are rather horseshoe-shaped than circular or elliptical. It is interesting, as an indication of pit-dwellings being contemporaneous with forts, a view will be shown in the sequel to be confirmed by other evidence, to note that there is a group of them in immediate proximity; half a dozen pits, indeed, being sheltered almost under the very walls of the fort.

Far more elaborate and complex in design, though otherwise identical in character with the three which have just been described, is the large Eastern Fort. The writer cleared it of the encumbering undergrowth, made a plan of it, and excavated such parts of the interior as seemed to promise any results. It proved to be of sufficient interest to warrant a detailed account.

If one looks eastward from the top of the slope, just behind the Rhodes farm, a bold ridge, nearly three miles away, shows clear cut against the sky. At its highest point, upon a knoll overgrown with shrubs and flowering trees, is

Inyanga.

Hill-forts.

the fort. Strategically, no more admirable site could have been chosen, and it much resembles those which Romans and ancient British marked out for their hill-camps in our own land. From the highest part all the other forts are plainly visible, and the view ranges to distant points many a mile beyond them. On the western and northern sides almost precipitous slopes defend the approach; eastwards the ground sinks less sharply; to the south the slope at first descends gradually, then falls abruptly to the little valley. Here a streamlet, fed by several tributary brooks, runs down to join the main Inyanga river, and a trench opening off it close to the main source deflected water in old days at a high level along the hill.

The most natural approach is from the western side, and on the way thither from the farm may be seen many of these dwellings, which have been erroneously termed "slave-pits," and will presently be more fully described. On the hillside itself these do not occur, but small circular enclosures are found within a few metres of the fort; as well as low walls which, so far as the tangled undergrowth admits of judging, were outworks or entrenchments like those observed round the Northern Fort.

The building itself is of irregular outline, as may be seen from the accompanying plan (Plate II. *a*). It is composed of six divisions, of which those lettered *A* and *B* stand on the level summit of the knoll, while the others are on the slopes, *C* in particular having a very sharp incline. The total want of symmetry in the plan is most conspicuous, and is characteristic of the spirit in which the entire work was executed. There is no uniform design; the building was evidently carried out by many hands working simultaneously at different points, and the resulting irregularities were compromised according to the inspiration of the moment. Thus, a wall was begun of a given thickness, but, on being carried to a certain point, came into collision with another wall, whereupon its thickness was reduced to meet the necessities of the new case. Even in *A*, which is the chief of the enclosures, and was probably the first to be built, the northern part of the wall is twice as thick as the southern. The divisions lettered as *C* and *D* are either due to an afterthought, or they are actually later constructions, though made by the same builders. They were both added piecemeal, and meet the outline of *F* and *E* without properly fitting it.

The exterior walls have bulged everywhere, and in several places have fallen. They average 2.50 m. in height, and, as in the other forts, are composed of two parts of about equal thickness, viz. an outer wall and a banquette running round inside, which is in this case about a metre lower. The

INYANGA

entrances are illustrated by the photograph in Plate I. b, left; they are just of Hill-forts. the height for a man to pass through in a stooping posture (average one metre high by 0.50 m. wide), and are roofed with lintels of single slabs resting upon the sides. Sometimes the entrances have been closed up again by a few stones placed on the outside, as may be seen in several places in the plan. Besides the entrances there are numerous loopholes in the wall (Plate I. b, right), some at about a quarter, others at about half its height above the ground. They are cut straight without any outward splay for the rake of a weapon, and vary from about 0.35 m. to about 0.50 m. square. Throughout the building the fitting of the stones is rough and inexact.[2]

Inside three of the divisions, viz. A, C, and D, there are small, low enclosures of more or less irregularly-circular or elliptical form, similar to those noted in the Northern and North-Eastern Forts. That they were built after, and not before, the exterior walls is evident from the way in which they are fitted in to the latter. They exactly resemble the circular and elliptical constructions found in the upper part of the pit-dwellings, and are made of unhewn boulders, rising in several courses to an average height of 0.70 m. or 0.80 m. from the ground. These were all excavated to the level of the bed-rock, which is here very close to the surface, and almost invariably yielded fragments of a coarse, hand-made, undecorated pottery. No other objects, however, were found in them, or anywhere within the precincts of the fort.[3]

On the Rhodes estate, and throughout the entire neighbourhood, are Pit-dwellings. found numbers of those curious buildings which, owing to a misconception of their character and purpose, are commonly spoken of as "slave-pits." Their nature has been generally misunderstood; too much attention has been concentrated on the most striking features, viz. the deep pit in the centre, with the roofed passage by which it is entered, while it has not been noticed that they are only two parts of what is really quite a complex structure. The word "structure" is used advisedly, for these are buildings in the proper sense of the term; the pit is not, as often supposed, sunk in the ground, but is raised up from it. The passage, again, is not a subterranean tunnel, but a corridor, of which the floor is everywhere level with the surface of the ground, while the side-walls and roof are above ground. Such pit-dwellings are almost invariably placed on a hillside or incline, and it is to this circumstance that they owe their peculiar appearance. For the builders deliberately utilised the fall of the ground to assist a special plan which they had in view. Starting from any suitable point on the hillside, they began to raise a massive

Inyanga.

Pit-dwellings.

platform, more or less circular or elliptical in form, of which the exterior face was composed of large unhewn blocks carefully selected and fitted (Plate V. *a*, to right of door), while the inside was filled with earth and rubble. When continuing this downhill, they did not simply maintain a uniform height, but added extra courses continually in proportion to the increase in the fall, so as to counteract the effect of the incline. So that, viewed in section, the platform would look like a wedge, of which the thick end is at the lower side of the slope. Consequently, the top surface is horizontal over its whole extent, whatever the level of the surrounding ground, and may be as much as two or three metres in height on its downhill side, though little more than one metre high where it begins. It is this peculiarity which made it possible to form, within the platform itself, a pit of perhaps 2.50 m. in depth and a passage descending into it, which runs underneath the top surface of the platform, while yet the floor of the pit and the floor of the passage are each exactly on the level of the outside ground. This may be appreciated from the sections in Plate IV., which illustrate similar buildings on a site to be described in the next chapter. But although the pit and the passage may first strike the attention, it is most important to realise that they are by no means the only component parts of the "pit-dwelling," as it should be termed. For the entire area of the built-up platform, which will be 20 metres in diameter in typical cases, is occupied by circular or elliptical enclosures, generally six besides the pit, and these are equally essential and indispensable to its completeness.

A particularly good example of a pit-dwelling, which may be seen hardly five minutes' walk from the Rhodes farm, is perfectly typical, and may be quoted as a standard for the purpose of description.

In Plate III. *a* is shown the ground-plan; Plate III. *b* is a photograph taken to illustrate various parts of the ground-plan; Plate IV. *b* is a section of the passage as it appeared when partly demolished, in order that the masonry might be studied; Plate IV. *a* is the lighting-hole for the passage, which is marked in the plan in the middle of the enclosure lettered *D*. In Plate V. *b* is seen the doorway of the passage leading into the pit as one looks at it from inside the pit; the interior of the passage is also visible, as its partial demolition had admitted some light; otherwise the passage would have been almost dark inside. In the plan the ellipse marked *C* is the pit. It is 2.40 m. deep on its southern and 2.70 m. deep on its northern side, the slope of the ground happening in this particular case to run south and north. Its north

INYANGA

wall is pierced at the ground-level by a small drain-hole measuring 0.80 m. by 0.40 m. The floor is paved with large slabs, unhewn, like all the other stones throughout the entire building; half of them were removed, but nothing was found beneath. The doorway which leads into the pit from the passage (Plate V. *b*) rises 1.20 m. from the floor to the under side of the lintel. The lintel itself is a slab 0.80 m. long by 0.20 m. thick, resting on the side walls as shown in the illustration, and so spanning a passage only 0.50 m. wide.

Pit-dwellings.

Let it now be supposed that we have climbed down into the pit from the top to investigate it. To climb out again would not be easy, so we will go through the passage, which would have been the orthodox way of entering the pit in the first instance. Passing under the lintel of the entrance, shown in Plate V. *b*, we find ourselves at once in a narrow, low corridor 0.50 m. wide and 1.20 m. high, that is to say, just large enough for a man to creep through, crouching all the way. The floor is one slab (0.15 m.) thick, and the roof is formed by a succession of slabs like the first. The masonry of the walls, though it appears rough at first sight, is very solid, and it is a task of considerable difficulty to dismantle them. The ground rises steeply, and accordingly the passage rises as we proceed and traverse the enclosure lettered *D* below its top surface. At about 4.00 m. after leaving the pit we arrive underneath a sort of manhole, shown in Plate IV. *a*, measuring in this case about 0.35 m. x 0.45 m., though it is often smaller. It was probably intended simply for lighting. After this point the passage makes a sharp turn of nearly half a right angle, which is less conspicuous in the plan, as the line of stones across the floor of *D* only roughly corresponds with the direction of the passage beneath. Passing under the southern wall of *D* we emerge on the upper side of the slope (Plate V. *a*). Outside the passage a single course of boulders forms, as shown in the plan (*E*), a sort of vestibule to the entrance.

Of the six enclosures which occupy the surface of the platform the most important is undoubtedly *D*, across which the corridor passes. The floor of *D* is sunk a few centimetres only below the top of the platform, and its western half is neatly paved with slabs, the eastern edge of this pavement being formed by the roof of the corridor, which is exactly flush with it except where (Plate IV. *a*) one or two extra stones are piled up to surround the lighting hole. The eastern half of *D* is unpaved, but built up solid with earth and boulders as high as the under side of the roof of the corridor.

The walls of *D*, and of the five other enclosures on the top surface,

Inyanga.

Pit-dwellings.

are very rudimentary in the pit-dwellings about the Rhodes farm. Their character may best be appreciated from the photograph in Plate III. *b*, which, being taken from the south-west corner behind *H*, shows the enclosures *H* and *G*, the passage *M*, which separates them from *D*, and a foreshortened view of *F*, with the two large boulders that mark its entrance. It can be seen that the walls are merely formed of one or two courses of quite rough, unhewn stones, laid without mortar, and not more than 0.50 m. to 0.60 m. in height. The purpose of these enclosures was betrayed by the objects found within them, which were all such as would be used in daily domestic life. Several of the articles so closely resemble what are used at the present day by the native blacks of the district, as to have raised a doubt whether they had not been deposited or dropped by Kaffirs using the old stone buildings as convenient resting-places. It will presently be shown, however, that there is no ground for this supposition, but that on the contrary there is every reason to believe the things found to be as old as the buildings themselves.

It may be as well, however, before entering on this question, to give details of the objects and the places in which they were found. In the building shown in Plate III. *a* fragments of household pottery, hand-made, and without decoration, were found a few centimetres below the surface of the block *Y*, which is not an enclosure, but merely a part of the general platform. At about the same level in *Y* were also found the scapula and teeth of an animal about the size of a goat and two damaged iron arrows, respectively 0.105 m. and 0.115 m. in length, perhaps of the type figured in Plate XII. No. 10. At the east end of the passage, between *Y* and *B*, just below the surface, was found an iron arrow 0.147 m. long (Plate XII. No. 11). In *A*, which is a circular enclosure with walls that rise 0.50 m. from the pavement, covering half its area, a piece of iron 0.055 m. long was found below the pavement, and another piece of iron 0.085 m. long just below the surface in the unpaved part. The second of these pieces was probably part of an arrow. In *B*, which was not, properly speaking, an enclosure, but rather a block of boulders and earth forming part of the platform, though carefully faced with picked stones where it fronted the passage at the north and east, were found two iron arrows. One was 0.140 m. long, of the shape shown in Plate XII. No. 11; the other was 0.130 m. long, and is shown in Plate XII. No. 12; both were found at a depth of 0.400 m. below the surface. At the same depth was found the forefoot of an animal. The circles marked as *K* and *L* were very slightly defined in the standard Inyanga dwelling, but in the Niekerk Ruins (see

INYANGA

Chap. II.) they were well and substantially built. In *L*, about 0.400 m. below the surface, was found a heavy armlet or anklet of solid bronze.

Pit-dwellings.

In *G* was found a fragment of a large household pot. The partition between *G* and *H* is made not of stone but of hard clay, in the style in vogue in Mashonaland. Just north of *H*, in the angle where the passage leads off the platform, was an ill-defined construction (not marked in the plan) which, from subsequent observations made upon another site, may probably be identified as a grain-shelter.

It has been much debated what was the purpose for which these pits were intended, and various conflicting views have been put forward. Some have maintained that they were merely for the housing of cattle; this suggestion may be confuted by the mere statement of the dimensions of the passage, which is too small for any cattle to pass through. Sheep or goats, indeed, might have been able to squeeze through, but even in a country where lions and leopards devour so much of the live stock it is difficult to suppose that the most enthusiastic farmer would have raised so elaborate a structure to defend his property while he himself went unprotected. In fact, it is almost impossible that this can have been the sole end to be served by buildings which it would take weeks to complete and which are finished with the utmost minuteness, for it must be observed that the entrance into a pit from its corridor is a masterpiece of dry building in stone. A favourite idea has been that the pit was intended for the imprisonment of slaves, who, it is said, would be unable to scale its steep sides, and would be driven in through the narrow winding passage. But this theory is open to exactly the same objections as the last, as well as to several others. Why should such care have been lavished upon a mere dungeon? It would not be necessary for the safe-keeping of slaves that the walls of the pit should be built with a fineness never shown in other parts of the building; it would not be necessary that a lighting hole should be put in their corridor and that their prison should be paved and provided with drainage holes. Every detail goes to show that the pit was distinguished from any of the other seven enclosures contained in the area of the platform by the special care and attention bestowed upon it. This fact by itself should be enough to prove that it was intended for the owners themselves to live in. Internal evidence alone, therefore, would suffice to confute the "slave-pit" theory. But it must further be remarked that here, as in so many other matters connected with the problems of the ancient ruins in Rhodesia, a theory has been advanced which rests on no foundation other than the merest *a priori*

Inyanga.

Pit-dwellings.

assumption, for we have no sufficient knowledge of the people who built these dwellings to allow us to state that they kept slaves at all. Not to weary the reader with other guesses, of which, perhaps, the best is that which would explain the pits as being storehouses for grain (a purpose to which the Mashonas of the present day sometimes actually adapt them), we may advance a view which is at any rate based on deduction from observed facts and on facts which have not hitherto been recorded. This is as follows :

The complex buildings which we have been describing, viz. massive platforms built against the slope of a hill, containing at the deeper end a pit which is entered by a narrow winding passage built within the platform, and on their top surfaces a series of low-walled enclosures connected by passages, are fortress dwellings. The pit is the heart of the building, and must have been inhabited either occasionally or regularly by its owners. The low enclosures on the surface were auxiliary dwellings, or it might be said rooms, in which the various industries and occupations of daily life were carried on. This was the explanation to which the writer was driven after considering all the others, and the reasons for adopting it will be fully detailed in the next chapter, which treats of a site where the pit-dwellings are found in their most complete and perfect form.

Irrigation trenches.

The country about Inyanga is well watered, but it would seem that the old inhabitants required a more general distribution of the supply than was afforded by the numerous streams running down from the hills. Accordingly, they adopted a practice which has been prevalent under similar conditions in several other countries, Algeria being one instance which has come under the writer's own observation. The stream was tapped at a point near its source, and part of the water deflected by a stone dam. This gave them a high-level conduit, by which the water could be carried along the side of a hill and allowed to descend more gradually than the parent stream. There are very many such conduits in the Inyanga region, and they often run for several miles. The gradients are admirably calculated, with a skill which is not always equalled by modern engineers with their elaborate instruments. The dams are well and strongly built of unworked stones without mortar; the conduits themselves are simple trenches about one metre in depth. The earth taken out of the trench is piled on its lower side and supported by boulders imbedded in it. In Plate XXXVI. *a* is an illustration of the southern part of the hill on which the Eastern Fort of Inyanga is placed. The centre of the photograph shows the stream, while high up on the left a line may be seen

PLATE I.

(a) ENTRANCES OF THE NORTHERN FORT, INYANGA. *See page* 4.

(b) MAIN WALL OF THE EASTERN FORT, INYANGA, FROM INSIDE. *See page* 7.

PLATE II.

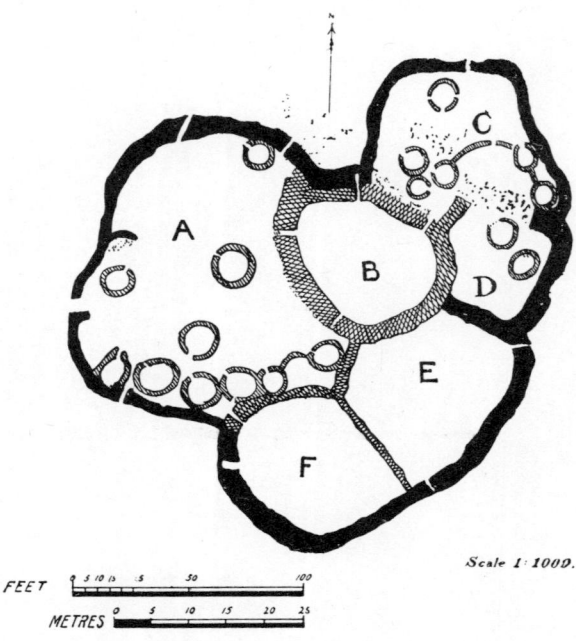

(a) PLAN OF EASTERN FORT AT INYANGA. See page 6.

(b) MAIN WALL OF THE EASTERN FORT, INYANGA, VIEWED FROM OUTSIDE.

See page 6.

PLATE III.

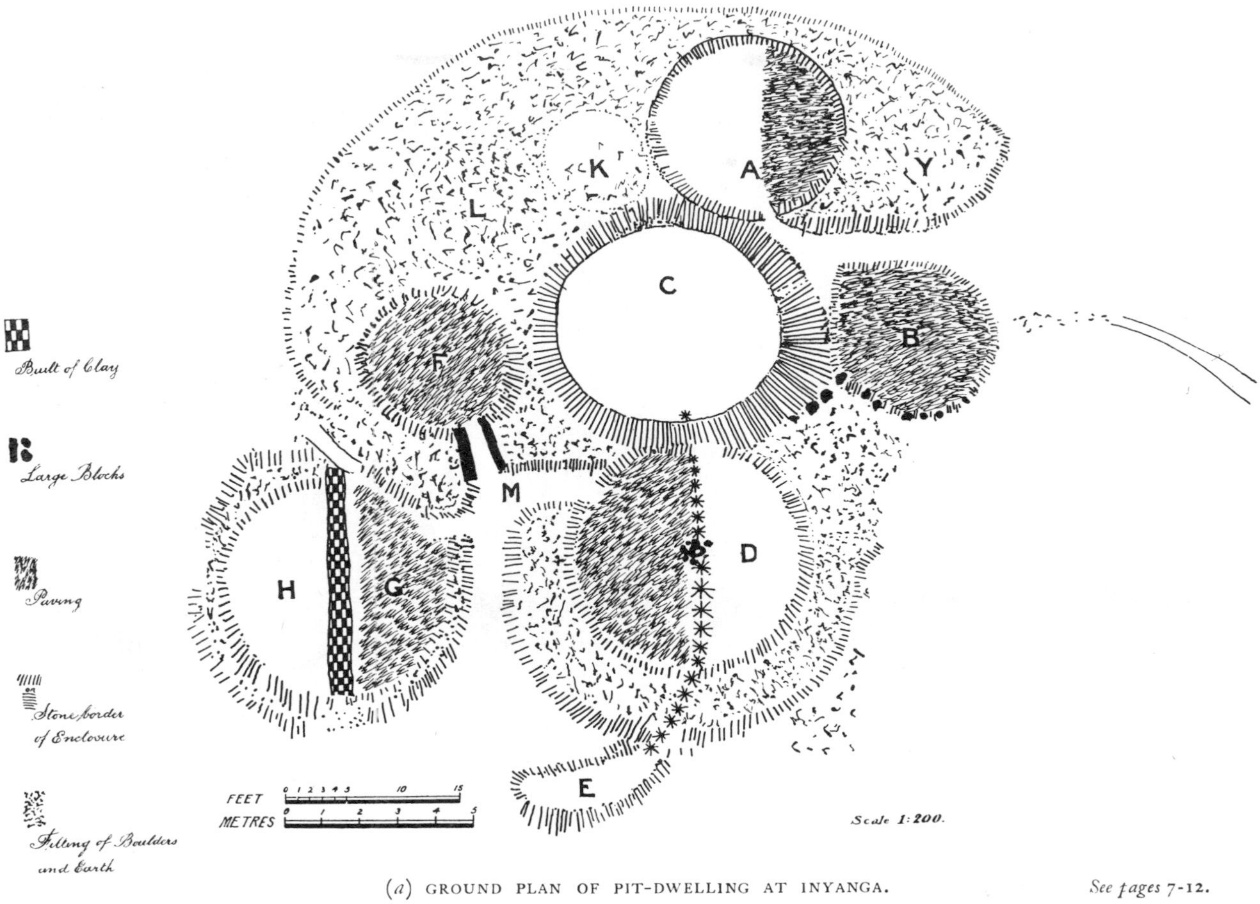

(a) GROUND PLAN OF PIT-DWELLING AT INYANGA. *See pages* 7-12.

(b) TOP SURFACE OF PART OF A PIT-DWELLING, INYANGA. *See page* 10.

PLATE IV.

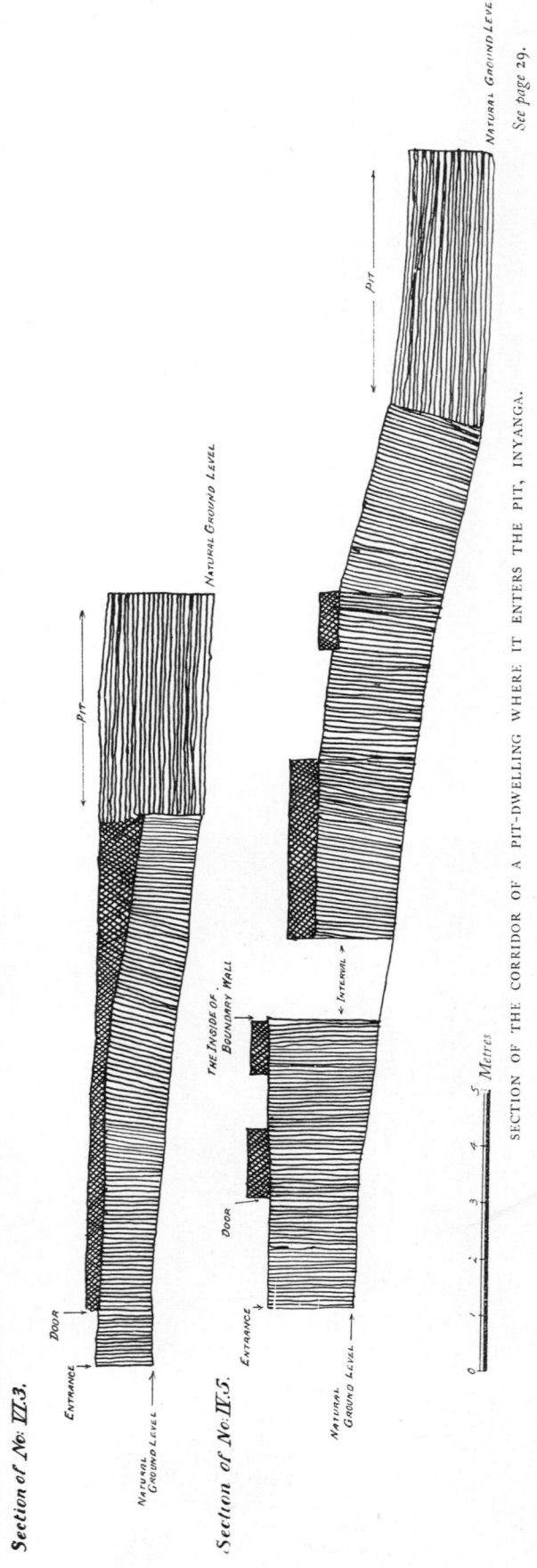

(a) LIGHTING-HOLE OF THE CORRIDOR OF A PIT-DWELLING, INYANGA. *See page 9.*

(b) DOORWAY OF THE CORRIDOR OF A PIT-DWELLING WHERE IT ENTERS THE PIT, INYANGA. *See page 9.*

PLATE V.

(a) PART OF A PIT-DWELLING, INYANGA. *See page* 9.

(b) DOOR AND CORRIDOR OF A PIT-DWELLING, INYANGA. *See page* 8.

running along the hillside. The latter is the water-trench which starts, at a point not shown in the photograph, just behind the slope. The illustration shows how in one place the trench, meeting rain-torrents pouring off the slope, has sapped the hill so as to cause a landslip, and it is worth remarking that such wash-outs sometimes occurred while the trench was still in use, for in this particular instance a new course had been dug several feet behind the original line to carry the water over the gap. At some points it is possible to see how the old engineers acted when they wished to alter the level of their conduit somewhat suddenly. They adopted the simple expedient of digging a pit, into which the water was conducted and then allowed to issue at the required depth.

Irrigation trenches.

There can be little doubt that the current explanation of these trenches as irrigation canals is correct. The only other imaginable use for them would have been as aqueducts to supply the forts and dwellings. But their topographical position excludes this hypothesis, for in most cases it would have been as easy to fetch the water from the stream itself as from the trench. No traces, indeed, remain of the cross-ditches which must once have run at right angles to such canals, but they would very soon have been obliterated if they were as small and unsubstantial as those, for instance, which the Egyptian fellah digs for the irrigation of his little plots.

We must suppose, therefore, that in past days Inyanga was a well-cultivated region, inhabited by a large and prosperous agricultural population. While they industriously tilled their land, however, the farmers felt themselves so little secure against the raids of other tribes, that even their dwellings were built with a view to defence against armed pillagers, while on the heights above were built forts which would serve as places of refuge when the homesteads were no longer tenable.

CHAPTER II

THE NIEKERK RUINS

Position of the ruins.

THE site which is to be described in this chapter is in some ways the most remarkable which has ever come under the writer's observation. It is no exaggeration to say that it extends over more than fifty square miles, and that there are few places within this large area where it is possible to walk ten yards without stumbling on a wall, a building, or an artificial heap of stones. "There has been as much labour expended here as on the building of the Pyramids, or even more," was the remark of a visitor.

The "Niekerk Ruins," as the writer wishes to name them, after Major P. van Niekerk, who guided him thither from Inyanga, have never been reported upon, and seldom visited save by an occasional hunter. The easiest way of reaching them from the Inyanga police-camp is by taking a straight line north-west in the direction of Matoko's kraal. This brings the traveller, after about ten miles of somewhat severe walking, to the great mountain, conspicuously higher than any other in the immediate neighbourhood, on the side of which is Dzambatsheka's Kraal. If he passes to the left or western slope of this mountain, which forms a landmark visible for miles, he will cross an easy nek and find himself at once in the heart of the ancient settlement.

General description.

The two photographs in Plate VI. will give a better idea of the general aspect of the site than any mere verbal description can convey. The great mountain is shown in Plate VI. *a* as it appears when viewed from a point about two miles to the north. It rises, perhaps, 2000 feet from the surrounding veldt, which is here only about 4000 feet above the sea-level, since the ten-mile walk from Inyanga has been downhill all the way. The lesser mountain immediately to the west of it may be seen in Plate VI. *b*. These two photographs were taken from the same standpoint, and are almost complementary to one another, for between the slope of the mountain on the right

THE NIEKERK RUINS

of Plate VI. *a* and the little kopje on the left of Plate VI. *b* there is an intervening space of only a few hundred yards. The nek by which the traveller is recommended to come is just discernible at the side of this little kopje. The photographs show innumerable lines running one behind the other over the whole ground. These are all built walls, row on row, covering plateau and hill alike so thickly that it is most fatiguing and difficult to make one's way across them. Almost everywhere where stones could rest they have been piled one upon another. The inaccessible upper cliff of the great mountain has necessarily been left untouched, but the lofty peak to the north of it (Plate VI. *a*, left) is walled to within a few feet of its summit. There is scarcely a stone, out of all the unimaginable millions in a tract more than eight miles long and six wide, that has not been handled by the builder.

General description.

An endless labyrinth without form or plan! is the first impression. Yet after many hours of stumbling up and down, over countless walls, past building after building, a certain system becomes apparent. If there are innumerable walls, they centre in more or less regular order about certain points, and the structures which they enclose repeat the same type again and again. At last one clear impression emerges, which is this:—There are nine or ten well-defined hills in the circle of view as one stands on a central point about two miles north of the great mountain. Each of these constitutes a separate unit, complete with its own buildings, and divided at the bottom from its neighbour by a boundary wall. Such a boundary is the first in a series of concentric lines which rise one behind the other, only a few feet apart, till the summit of the hill is attained. Then, arrived on the top of the ridge, after mounting over sometimes only thirty, sometimes fifty or more, of these girdle-lines, the explorer finds himself in the heart of the village which its ancient inhabitants made so difficult of access. Here he is confronted with circular buildings, which he recognises at once as of the same pattern as those pit-dwellings which were described in the last chapter.

This is the general scheme of arrangement, but of course there are many variations of detail, most of which are due to the configuration of the ground in particular places. For instance, the walls, though concentric, are irregular, as it was the habit of the builders always to follow the natural trend of the hill and to adapt their plan accordingly. If a great rock offered a natural buttress the line of wall would be carried out or in to meet it, and symmetry of outline was always sacrificed to convenience. Had the hills been perfectly round, the girdle-walls would have formed concentric circles; as it is, they

Niekerk Ruins. General description.

wind in and out in serpentine fashion, but at quite definite intervals, from one another. At the foot of the slope they may be several metres apart and only a course or two high; further up they draw nearer together and are higher, till at the top they will be only 2.0 m. apart and as much as 2.0 m. in height. In most parts of the site the building is identical in style with that noted in the last chapter, viz. rough, dry building without mortar; but in districts of the eastern hills, which were perhaps taken into occupation later than the others, mortar has been used intermittently, though the stones are nowhere dressed or hewn. Again, in several parts, and especially on the eastern hills, the unity of design has been broken owing to another cause, viz. that small knolls or kopjes crop out from the hillside, and each of these has been treated as a unit in itself, so that, while there is a general system of entrenchment for the entire main hill, yet within this there are several subordinate series of walls ringing round each prominent point.

To make an adequate surveyor's plan of so vast an area would have demanded at least as many months as there were days available. The next best thing seemed to be to study the site according to the natural divisions which the builders themselves had followed, and to describe these one by one. But the account of them must be somewhat curtailed here to avoid a wearisome repetition of small details. Now, therefore, that the reader may be presumed to have grasped the general idea of the Niekerk Ruins, it may be most practical to conduct him over so much of them as a sturdy walker may visit in a few hours, selecting the chief buildings and points of interest for special notice.

Division VI. of the ruins.

Starting, then, from the nek between the two mountains, and descending from the kopjes shown on the left of Plate VI. *b*, the visitor should direct his course to the north-north-west. He will first of all traverse a strip of ground seamed with little watercourses, which is to be dealt with at length in the next chapter, and if he follows any one of the stream beds he will arrive at (620 metres) a finely-built pit-dwelling, which will be referred to as N. VI. 3.* It is precisely of the same type as those described in the last chapter, a massive structure of unhewn stones built upon sloping ground. On the lower side of the slope the face of the platform is 1.50 m. high,

A pit-dwelling.

---

* N. standing for Niekerk Ruins, VI. for the sixth division of the ruins, 3 for the third building in that division. The numbering of each building of Division VI. has been painted upon it, either over the entrance or in some other conspicuous place.

and the enclosures erected upon it average 0.50 m. in height. The pit is, as usual, elliptical rather than circular in outline, and measures 5 metres in maximum external diameter by 2 metres in depth. The corridor, which leads into the pit, has its vestibule on the west side, so that the aspect of the building is not identical with that of the standard type as planned in Plate III. *a*, but it is amply clear, from scores of examples, that the orientation of these dwellings was determined by nothing but mere convenience. The several parts may be denominated by the same letters as those used in Plate III. *a*. In *E* the vestibule of the corridor, at about 1 metre in front of the point where it first passes under the enclosure lettered *D*, was found a hand-made bowl of plain red pottery (Plate X. No. 6) buried mouth downwards. In the centre of the corridor itself, that is to say, underneath *D*, were found two more broken bowls, as well as fragments of a larger vessel, and a piece of animal bone, which might possibly have served as an implement. In *H* was found a piece of iron, probably a broken arrow, and in a sort of annexe, corresponding in position to the supposed grain-hut of the Inyanga pit-dwelling, were the iron arrow figured in Plate XII. No. 10 and two shapeless fragments of iron. From *F* came fragments of pots, one of which was ornamented with an incised chevron, and another with an incised lattice pattern. In *K* there stood a large triangular slab of stone, supported upon four small blocks. It measured 1.20 m. × 0.85 m. maximum length and maximum breadth, was raised 0.17 m. from the ground, and closely resembled the stones on which meal is ground in modern Makalanga huts. Beneath it, buried a few centimetres under the ground, were fragments of rough hand-made pottery, parts of the shin-bones of an animal, and a piece of iron which had probably been part of an arrow. Between *B* and *C* runs a passage, in which a half-ring of iron, like that figured in Plate XII. No. 5, was found.

A pit-dwelling.

The plan of N. VI. 3 is, as has been stated, that of the standard type, with its pit and corridor and six enclosures upon the surface. But whereas the dwellings on the Rhodes estate were completed by a plain girdle-wall, there are here supplementary outer precincts. On the southern side, for instance, the wall is extended to partly enclose an elliptical stone structure of a kind not hitherto observed, but by no means infrequent on this site. The writer was inclined to regard these as altars, and destroyed three in the hope of finding votive objects in or around them. His search, however, was not rewarded by anything more valuable than two quartz arrow-heads, one of rough workmanship being actually within the masonry, the other, a finer

Altars?

Niekerk Ruins.

Altars?

specimen, about a metre outside. Fragments of rough pottery, however, occurred both within the masonry and under the surrounding soil. The conjectured altars vary in size, but may be said to average about 6.0 m. × 3.50 m., or 4.0 m. in length and breadth, by 2.0 m. in height. They are well faced with undressed but carefully selected blocks, within which the core is a rubble of small pebbles and earth.

On the north side the two girdle-walls of N. VI. 3 are prolonged into what looks at first sight like a sort of avenue or road, but is actually the western boundary of the division called N. VI. in this scheme. This avenue, 3.50 m. wide, traverses ground unencumbered by buildings, and, if the windings are discounted, runs a little east of north. At 190 metres a cross-path leads off to the left, but it is better to pass this and go on to where, 100 metres farther on, a second cross-path turns away to the right. Another 90 metres along the avenue would have brought us to the crest of the hill where N. VI. 16 stands, but we prefer to turn off and inspect N. VI. 4, 60 metres away.

Types of building other than pit-dwellings.

In Plate VIII. *a* is a plan of N. VI. 4, which shows it to belong to a different class from any of the buildings viewed hitherto, though characteristic enough of the site. There are, indeed, several of these somewhat featureless enclosures on the southern side of Division VI., as well as on the top of the hill. Some of them look more like workshops than habitations, and, though enclosed within a widely ramifying system of walls, are not, like N. VI. 3, miniature citadels. But though the ground-plan is modified, the general style is the same that is found all over these ruins, viz. a combination of curved walls of rough unmortared stone-work, forming enclosures of irregularly elliptical shape, which are divided by other curved walls or by low rings of boulders into various compartments. The exterior wall of N. VI. 4 is 1.50 m. high, the divisional walls are lower, viz. 1.30 m., 0.90 m., and even 0.50 m., at various points. Of the compartments lettered *A* and *D* there is nothing particular to remark; while *C* is a small pit within the thickness of the exterior wall, the existence of which cannot be explained; it was dug to the foundation without giving any clue. Between *D* and *E* is a passage roofed with stone slabs, like the corridors of the pit-dwellings and the entrances of the forts. In the sides of this passage two holes have been left opposite to one another, evidently to receive a wooden bar which would be slid to and fro. Such bars were actually found in position within a fort to be described below. It might seem superfluous to put a roofed and barred entrance where there is apparently easy access over more than one open space or low line of stones, but it must always be remembered that what is now visible within these enclosures amounts to nothing more than the foundations of dwellings and rooms which once stood there. For it is quite evident that the rings of stones both here and on the platforms of the pit-dwellings were mere supports for circles of stakes roofed with a thatching of grass. That is to say, the people who lived in these ruins built their houses and shelters exactly like the modern Kaffirs, although they surrounded them with girdle-walls and entrenchments, unlike any which are made at the present day. It may be remarked in passing that there is no evidence of modern natives having squatted on the site, and that in any case the same characteristics are repeated over so wide an area that no hypothesis of modern occupation will explain them away. The enclosure, N. VI. 4, may be compared in several points to modern kraals. The partition of hardened clay across *E*, like that in the Inyanga pit-dwelling (Plate III. *a*), is invariably found in the huts of the Makalanga, and the circular platforms lettered *F*, *G*, and *H* are highly suggestive of hut foundations. It is worth while to give particular attention to *F*, *G*, and *H*, as they are the first instances of a form of construction which will frequently recur. They are 3 or sometimes 4 metres in diameter. A section from top to bottom would show 0.20 m. of earth containing numerous fragments of charcoal, beneath which is a paving of stone slabs 0.10 m. thick, supported on pillars of rough stone 0.30 m. high. Several stones hollowed out by grinding meal upon them were to be seen in the building. One, 0.40 m. long by 0.30 m. wide, and set in a clay frame 0.10 m. thick, stood in the eastern half of the subdivision lettered *E*, where no other objects were found. Iron implements were unearthed at several points, viz. half way between *F* and *H*, the triangular axe figured in Plate XII. No. 7; in *B* three straight pieces, two of which were not unlike those figured in Plate XII. No. 3, while the third is given in Plate XII. No. 15, as well as sherds of pottery and a split animal bone. These occurred just below the surface of the soil, which is only a few centimetres deep over the bed-rock. The half-ring of iron like that in Plate XII. No. 5 was found in *G* below the level of the platform.

As may be seen from the indications on the plan, N. VI. 4 is by no means isolated, but is continuous with another series of buildings, N. VI. 5, the boundary-wall of which touches its eastern side. On the south it is protected by low parallel walls past which we go on turning down at the south-east corner to descend the roadway outlined by the girdle-walls of N. VI. 4 and N. VI. 5

Niekerk Ruins.

Continuation of tour round Division VI.

respectively. At 35 metres from the corner we reach the end of the roadway, and bear in an eastward direction, the objective being N. VI. 10, a building of which Plate VIII. *b* shows the plan. To arrive there it is necessary first to cross 12 lines of low walls forming terraces of gradually increasing breadth, after which (100 metres from the roadway) appears N. VI. 6, one of a little group of enclosures closely adjoining each other. The first, N. VI. 6, is of very irregular outline, the exterior wall (1 metre thick) being really made up of a series of arcs of ellipses joined up. Its diameter * in the axis by which we have approached is 19.0 m., and the interior arrangement may be described as follows:—A circular platform interrupts the line of the western wall, then 5.0 m. from the wall begins a circle of one course of boulders about 2.30 m. in diameter, by the side of which is a grindstone, and adjoining it on the left another little circle. The latter abuts on a large circle, 6.30 m. in diameter, formed of one and of two courses of boulders which rise 0.40 from the ground and make a wall 0.80 m. thick. This occupies the exact centre of the enclosure; the south-east corner is filled by a small horse-shoe construction, and on the north-west side is the usual lintelled entrance. On the west of N. VI. 6 a series of walls 1.0 m. high leads to N. VI. 5, and on the east low lines of stones connect at a few metres with N. VI. 7, in which the only point to be specially noted is the way in which the circular clay platforms are fitted in to the peculiar curves of the wall, which was obviously built at the same time as them. In this building was found a piece of iron (Plate XII. No. 16), and just outside it three characterless iron fragments.

Immediately in front, some 42.0 m. away, and across six lines of walls, is the building N. VI. 10, of which the ground-plan is exhibited in Plate VIII. *b*. It is unquestionably a habitation, but belongs to a class of which no clear example has hitherto occurred. While the distribution of its parts is apparently derived from that of the pit-dwelling, yet the fortress character which distinguishes the latter has disappeared. Connecting links between the two types are supplied by several enclosures in Divisions IV. and VII. of the Niekerk Ruins, and the essential difference between them may be expressed in a single sentence. For the several compartments of a pit-dwelling are placed in and upon an artificial platform, whereas in the class of building represented by N. VI. 10 they are built immediately upon the unlevelled surface of the rock. Consequently, of course, pit and corridor disappear, and the ground-plan is correspondingly modified. But two of the principal features of a pit-

---

* The diameters given in this chapter are always *interior* diameters unless the contrary is explicitly stated.

THE NIEKERK RUINS

dwelling are always retained, viz. the main central circle (*D*) and the lintelled entrance, here closed by a wooden bar, the sockets for which are visible, though the wood has perished.

Continuation of tour round Division VI.

The interior of N. VI. 10 is divided into a number of compartments and recesses, some of which are clearly defined by low walls, while others are barely indicated by scattered boulders. All the divisional lines have been reproduced as closely as possible in the plan, and it can be seen how every foot of space has been utilised for a hut-foundation, a shelter, or a niche. The partitions are sometimes so rudimentary that they can hardly be described as *built*, but, as already remarked, they were never more than supports for perishable erections of wood and straw which have been burned or otherwise destroyed in the course of time. The exterior wall rises 1.50 m. to 2.0 m., and the better of the interior divisional walls rise 1.0 m. from the ground. The lintel of the entrance is 1.10 m. from the floor and 0.20 m. thick; over it are two more courses of slabs, making a further 0.45 m. of height. Evidence of human occupation was abundant, broken household pottery being found in *A*, *C*, *F*, *G*, *H*, and *K*, while in *G* there was also found a fragment of iron. In *L* stood seven narrow, upright stones, which probably once supported a slab for the grinding of meal.

Another 50 metres down the hill a series of four walls has been lettered N. VI. 11, and just beyond them, following the course of the valley bottom, is a substantial rampart, the boundary of Division VI. on this side. Immediately across the stream the entrenchments take a different trend, to form a fresh system defending the kopjes under the great mountain. We follow the course of the stream-bed and girdle-wall for about 90 metres, then turn where they bend due north, and walk 250 metres to a point which is abreast of the axis of the hill on which Division VI. is placed. Above us rise all its outworks tier upon tier, and on the right begin the first lines of another hill. A sharp turn to the west and the ascent begins. It is a steep climb, over no less than 37 successive walls. At first they are wide apart and low, then they draw together and rise higher, till towards the top of the ridge they are 1.50 m. and 2.0 m. high, and scarcely 2.0 m. apart.

The first enclosure on this side is N. VI. 12, a ruined dwelling evidently dismantled before the desertion of the settlement. The main circle (*D*) still stands, and there are the remains of a lintelled door. The dwelling was probably of the same class as N. VI. 10, and measured 16.0 m. in diameter. Its girdle-walls include further a small horse-shoe enclosure 8.50 m. in length,

Niekerk Ruins.

Continuation of tour round Division VI.

within which stands one of the elliptical heaps conjectured to be altars. Immediately adjoining is a diminutive circle only 3.0 m. in diameter, beyond which again is a fresh series of entrenchments running north and south. Past these is another horse-shoe enclosure surrounding an altar-like heap (N.VI.14), and a few paces behind it is N.VI.15, a dwelling of the N.VI.10 type.

So far we have been ascending the whole time since the valley bottom, but now a few more paces brings us to N.VI.16 on the crown of the hill. In plan this is somewhat anomalous, as may appear from Plate IX., where it is drawn. That the building served for human habitation is proved by the objects found in and just outside it, viz. a pottery bowl, two potsherds with incised patterns, and the soapstone object figured in Plate XII. No. 24, which resembles what modern natives use as the counterpart of the classical strigil. Besides these were found flat pieces of iron which may possibly be fragments of an adze or hoe. From the adjoining N.VI.17 came a piece of copper (Plate XII. No. 20) tastefully ornamented with an incised chevron placed point to point. The construction of N.VI.17 is interesting for one peculiarity, which is that the existing entrance runs askew to another built exactly like the corridor of a pit-dwelling. The original intention must have been to make a regular pit-dwelling, but it may be doubted whether the intention was ever fulfilled. However, there are undoubtedly some instances (see p. 27 and the plan of II. 7 in Plate IX.) which prove that pit-dwellings were occasionally converted into buildings of the other class. Of course, it is unnecessary to attribute the alterations of plan to any but the ancient inhabitants, for even the secondary constructions are in no way different from scores of other buildings on the site, which are certainly contemporary with the oldest existing there.

The types of buildings found in Division VI.

It appears, then, that several of the buildings in Division VI. have been dismantled; that there are two typical forms of dwelling which occur there, the first of which, viz. pit-dwellings, or miniature citadels, are rarer there than in some other parts of the site, and, lastly, that some of these latter have been converted from their original design. The probable inference is that the occupants of this district, close under the impregnable mountain, and within a few hundred yards of the fortified kopjes, felt secure enough to dispense with some of the precautions which their less fortunately situated neighbours considered essential to their safety.

Division II.

The Sixth Division has perhaps been sufficiently explored for the present purpose, so we may descend its northern side, without pausing to note details,

THE NIEKERK RUINS

and go straight to the Second Division, N. II., the eastern extremity of which is **Division II.** formed by the steep eminence which fronted us across the valley from the point where we stood just now. The kopje in question is the central point of the Niekerk Ruins, or at least of so much of them as can be dealt with here. It commands a magnificent view of all the surrounding hills, and is itself plainly visible from the western side of the great mountain. To any one who starts from the nek between the two mountains the kopje bounding N.II. shows up about a mile and a half away and about 10 degrees west of north.* In order to reach it from the top of N.VI. some sixteen entrenchment lines must be crossed on the downhill slope, after which we arrive at the northern girdle-wall of N.VI. and turn to the right along the roadway which it forms at the valley bottom. At 90 metres along this roadway is a cross-path to the right formed by the eastern girdle-wall of N.II. abutting on the western wall of N.V., but we pass it by. Immediately on the left front rises the kopje, and it will be advisable to take the shortest cut to the top, even though that involves the scaling of many walls. Once there a complete panorama of the whole site **Panoramic view from** may be enjoyed. First, looking towards the north and north-west, a long ridge, **kopje in** perhaps a mile distant, across a wide valley, bounds the view and forms Division **Division II.** I. (N. I.) in the present arrangement. The kopje where we now stand, with the adjoining high ground, is to be N.II., or the Second Division. Below it, on the east, is the valley which starts from the northern slope of the great mountain, and widening gradually, is joined by the lateral valley separating the Second Division from the First. A mile away, east-north-east, on the opposite side of the main valley, is a wooded hill with numerous lines visible even from here. This is Division III., behind which, on the horizon, are seen the mountains near Nani. The range beyond Division III. lies outside the limits of this account, so Division IV. is all that nearer district to the south-east of III., where slopes, interrupted by outcropping knolls, run up to the peaks north-east of the mountain.

Turning round to the side by which we have ascended we see the great mountain that dominates the whole settlement, rising, perhaps, 2000 feet from the surrounding ground; and, due south from where we stand, the lesser mountain beside it. At our feet extends a wide stretch of low ground cut up by innumerable lines of walls (see Plate VI. *a*) which bend round to the left

---

* *Magnetic* north, as are all the observations given in this volume. The compass bearings given in Chaps. I. and IV. were taken in the month of April, those in this chapter in the month of May, the remainder in June and July, except for Khami, which was not explored till August.

24 MEDIÆVAL RHODESIA

Niekerk Ruins.

Panoramic view from kopje in Division II.

to enclose a low eminence. All this is Division V., a region which contains little of interest. Where its girdle-wall meets that of the neighbouring western hill begins Division VI. (see Plate VI. *b*), while the plateau to the west of this again, directly between us and the lesser mountain, is called Division VII. The plateau slopes westward to low ground, beyond which, three miles from our present standpoint, and scarcely separable at that distance, are two ridges which complete the circuit of the compass and may be numbered as VIII. and IX., though they will not be described in the text. The settlement at the Niekerk Ruins may challenge a more famous capital in respect of the number of its hills.

Modifications of the pit-dwelling.

After obtaining this bird's-eye view of the ground to be studied we may investigate Division II., which offers some new points of considerable interest. In the eastern brow stands an elliptical enclosure (N.II. 1), 12.0 m. in diameter, with ruined entrance and passage, 35 metres to the west of which is another small building which need not be particularly noticed. At 100 metres west of this again is a pit-dwelling, N.II. 2, 17.0 m. in diameter, which affords the first example of the *discontinuous* corridor. That is to say, the corridor in this case is *above* the level of the platform, and does not begin until 2 metres after the exterior wall has been passed. So that N.II. 2 is a definite connecting link between the two types of habitation noted in Division VI.; it is the pit-dwelling in which some of the distinguishing peculiarities are already modified.

The fort in Division II.

On the western edge of the hill, 110 metres from this point, is the most interesting building in the whole division, a true fort (N.II. 3), placed in a position of great natural strength. The ground-plan is simple, one irregular ellipse enclosing another of less diameter, which abuts upon it in such a way that a single wall serves the two for a considerable distance (cf. diagram on Plate XIII. *a*). The innermost is 16.0 m. in maximum by 9.0 m. in minimum diameter, while the containing outer enclosure measures 25.0 m. × 24.0 m., so that it is nearly circular. The general style of construction is identical with that of the forts upon the Rhodes estate. The exterior walls average 1.50 m. in thickness, including the usual banquette, and rise in places 2.50 m. from the ground. As at Inyanga, the great boulders imbedded in the hillside are utilised, and the masonry is carried over them. There are three entrances in the outer wall, precisely similar to those at Inyanga, and a fourth leads from the outer to the inner enclosure. It is in this last entrance that the wooden bar is still preserved almost intact in its original place. It is a plain beam, flat in section,

THE NIEKERK RUINS

1.80 m. in length by 0.090 m. in greatest breadth, laid horizontally across the passage and running in socket-holes left for the purpose in the walls. The one socket-hole is 0.60 m. deep; the other, in which the beam was intended to rest when shot back to leave the passage open, is 1.50 m. deep. The bar must have been built in while the walls were actually being erected, for it is impossible to withdraw it in the space that is now available. The passage which it closes is 2.0 m. long and 1.15 m. high, and the bar is placed at 1.50 m. from the outer end, about half-way up between floor and lintel. That the wood, which is apparently mahobo-hobo, should have survived in such perfect preservation is most remarkable. But this is not the only instance, for close beside the northern entrance of the outer wall was lying a partially burned beam which, although no longer in place, had evidently served as the bar for that door. The majority of buildings in the Niekerk Ruins had once been closed in the same way, but though the socket-holes are to be seen the wood has disappeared; which, considering the annual bush fires and other chances of destruction, is only what would be expected. The only other point to be remarked before quitting the fort is that most of the outer enclosure is occupied by circular platforms, in which were found some sherds of pottery and pieces of iron.

The fort in Division II.

Another and not less interesting fort stands exactly opposite in the middle of the hill called N.I. The easiest route to it is to start from the southern slope of N.I. after leaving the first fort and crossing the swampy valley. Looking back from the side of N.I. there is a characteristic view of Divisions II. and VII., the foreground being occupied by the valley as it trends southward to meet the invisible Inimgombwe river. Half-way up the ascent, and south of the knoll, which is crowned by the fort, are several rather anomalous dwellings, the plan of one of which (N.I. 1) is shown in Plate IX. The site of the stronghold itself has been chosen with the unerring judgment that characterises all the strategical dispositions of the old builders. The only fairly accessible side is protected by close rows of walls, and it is a severe climb to the summit. The plan is a development of and improvement upon that of the first fort (cf. diagram in Plate XIII. *a*). A main enclosure, irregularly elliptical, and about 43 metres in maximum length, is divided into halves by a curved wall across its lesser axis. Inside the southern of the divisions so formed is built an inner enclosure, 11.50 m. in diameter from north to south, and standing free of the outer wall in such a way as to leave a passage about

Division I.

The fort.

Niekerk Ruins. Division I. The fort. two metres wide between the two suggesting the origin of the well-known "Parallel Passage" at Zimbabwe. There is only one door in the exterior wall, and each of the two inner enclosures is entered in succession from the outer through its own door. The northern half of the fort is occupied by several circular platforms; its single surrounding wall is 3 metres thick, and in places 3 metres high. The stone-laying is very rough, but much dexterity has been shown in dovetailing the living rocks, one of which towers up fully 6 metres, into the circuit of the rampart.

The military considerations which determined the type of dwelling. From the fort there is a pleasant walk of about a mile along the axis of the ridge, unembarrassed for once by walls. The old settlers apparently considered themselves already safe enough within their outer lines and close to the sheltering fastness, and only dwellings are to be seen here. Indeed, as was hinted before, the different parts of the site vary considerably in respect of the degree of their entrenchment. For whereas Divisions V., VI., and VII. are comparatively weakly protected, yet in VIII. and IX. the rings of defence are continued over the very last metre of free ground, and in parts of IV. there are fifty or sixty successive ramparts between the valley and the top of the hill. No doubt the chief consideration was the neighbourhood or distance of a secure place of refuge. The occupants of the Fifth, Sixth, and Seventh Divisions were within easy reach of the kopjes under the mountain, and had converted them into very formidable castles, while those of the First and Second were provided with their own particular forts. But IV., VIII., and IX. were outlying settlements, which might very possibly have nothing to trust to but their own individual strength. It may be remarked in passing that IV. may well be a little later in date than the more central parts, and that in IV. alone was mortar used—it is true only spasmodically—in the building.

Return to Division II. The northern end of Division I. is the most distant point to be visited on this occasion, and now we retrace our steps to the fort on the eastern edge of Division II. Thence we shall take another route home, in order to visit two or three places which are instructive as explaining certain features that have recurred in the description of dwellings.

Close under the shelter of the fort are numerous walls and enclosures. About 200 metres south of it, not pausing to examine a number of buildings which exhibit a few more details, we turn sharp to the right and follow the **Another type of hut foundation.** axis of the ridge. Some 100 metres in this direction, past one or two enclosures of no special interest, is a plain enclosure (N.II. 5) which is well worth attention, as it gave the first positive proof of the character of those circular platforms which were first observed in N. VII. 4 and have been so constantly noted since. They stand ordinarily a few inches above the level of the enclosure floor, upon a number of small upright blocks, and are paved with stone slabs, upon which rests a layer of hard clay. Their diameter averages 3 to 4 metres.

Another type of hut foundation.

As the result of digging in two or three places it appeared that fragments of charred wood are usually embedded in the clay of the floor; iron implements were more than once found below it, and in one case there was an animal bone among the upright slabs supporting the platform. Grinding stones are usually found in close proximity to them. By some happy chance the platforms in N. II. 5 had preserved what had not been detected in any of those previously noted. They were strewn with fragments of burned red clay, which were fluted by the cast of something which had lain in or against them. The flutings were about an inch in diameter, some running vertically, some horizontally. A careful search detected a piece in which horizontal and vertical lines were combined, and it was then at once evident that the flutings were the cast of wattled woodwork. In short, the pieces of clay were fragments of the walls which had once stood upon the platforms, and these walls had been made exactly as the modern Kaffir makes them, viz. of a circle of stakes, strengthened by wattle lashings inside and outside, against which thick clay is plastered, so as generally to hide the wattle-work.

These fragments of walls were subsequently found in a good many cases. There can be no doubt, therefore, what is the meaning of clay-floored platforms on the Niekerk Ruins, and it is well to clearly understand it thus early, as it is the key to much that will be described in later chapters.

About 90 metres beyond this, in the same line along the axis of the hill, is the only other building to which particular attention need be directed, N. II. 7 (figured in Plate IX.). The details of the plan will sufficiently explain its nature. A pit-dwelling once stood there, and half of it remains in the small semicircle shown in the right-hand corner. But it had fallen into ruins, or had been dismantled, and the girdle-wall had been extended to make space for a dwelling of the derivative type, without pit or corridor, in which the most noticeable feature is the number of circular platforms.

We return to N. VI. 3 (the first building viewed on this tour) by way of N. VII., a division which is well worth visiting, but which it would take too long to describe in full. In Plate IX. are shown the plans of some unusual forms of building from this Division. That lettered N. VII. 3 is a diminutive

Niekerk Ruins.

pit-dwelling of very simple form, in the corridor of which was found a pot inverted over one or two bones of a very young infant, the only case in which any human remains were discovered. The other two buildings, N.VII. 1 and N.VII. 2, have no pits.

Summary of results obtained from a study of the Niekerk Ruins.

To summarise the results of this long and perhaps tedious chapter, which, however, gives the shortest possible epitome of a complex and difficult investigation, we have, it may be hoped, learned somewhat of the history implicit in the Niekerk Ruins. They were inhabited by a people who must have lived in perpetual apprehension of attack, and therefore protected themselves behind one of the vastest series of entrenchment lines to be found anywhere in the world. For the ruins described in this chapter do not by any means exhaust the area covered by fortifications. Every hill that can be seen northward from the farthest point here described is ringed with walls. Where the hills melt away into the low veldt they disappear, but it is said they are resumed again at Nani.* Southwards, as we have seen, forts and pit-dwellings extend over the whole of the Inyanga district for a considerable distance, and the forts at least are found down the road to Rusapi, and in the other direction almost as far as Penhalanga.

No foreign influences.

The people who built here were of African origin, and evidently akin to the race from which the present inhabitants have sprung, for their dwellings show the same fundamental ideas of construction, and many of their implements and articles of daily use are identical with those found amongst the modern inhabitants of the country. They were not affected by either Oriental or European influences, for no single object of other than genuinely African character has been found where they lived, and all characteristics of European or Saracen architecture are conspicuously absent.

The next chapter will supply the material by which to judge more fully of the nature of their arts and industries; this has been devoted more particularly to their dwellings, and may fitly close with one or two remarks upon them.

The various types of buildings.

The buildings observed on the Niekerk Ruins are of three main types—forts, miniature citadels, and walled dwellings which have not the character

---

* These entrenchments have been erroneously described as irrigation terraces by those who have only seen the lower series and the bottoms of the hills. No one, however, who explores them thoroughly can doubt their real nature. The view that they were made for purposes of cultivation would be untenable in any case. There is not enough water to irrigate, the walls are too high, except close down to the valleys, to allow of crops growing between them, nor is there any indication that soil has washed out from them. At the most a few small crops may have been grown between the lower tiers, but the immediate connection of the walls with the pit-dwellings and forts is quite unmistakable.[4]

THE NIEKERK RUINS

of citadels. Besides these, there are numerous enclosures, the nature of which cannot be wholly explained, but which belong very probably to the category of workshops, and sometimes, perhaps, of cattle kraals.

The various types of buildings.

The forts have been sufficiently described. Of the miniature citadels, that is to say, the pit-dwellings, a great deal has already been said, but one or two points have still to be treated. The first of these is the question, what purpose did the pit itself serve? Several theories have been already examined and rejected. Two things at least are clear, the first that the pit is the very centre, or kernel, of the whole system of fortification when it stands on a fortified hill; the second that it was at any rate occasionally inhabited. The only explanation that seems to fit the circumstance is that the pit was the last refuge whenever the defenders were hard pressed in siege. The fighting men, of course, would not go there—it would have been a veritable death-trap,—but, like some of the modern Kaffirs, they thought at once of a place to keep their women in safety. Here in the fort they would be out of reach of flying missiles, and the narrow corridor could be defended by the very last man.

Lastly, it remains to show how another type of habitation was developed from the pit-dwelling. When there was no longer any necessity for fortifying the actual home, that is to say, whenever a fort or a walled kopje was close to hand, the inhabitants of the settlement abandoned the citadel type and adopted a less costly and troublesome style of building. But there were several stages in the process, and many intermediate forms may be observed. The first step was, while retaining the corridor, to omit the piling up of stone against it; thus the platform naturally tended to disappear. Then only a discontinuous corridor was used (cf. section in Plate IV.). Finally, the corridor was regarded as altogether superfluous, and no platform being built, no pit was constructed. And so the citadel-dwelling was replaced by another form, which, however, reproduces the same general arrangement and distribution of parts in the ground-plan, though wholly different if viewed in section. Gradually even the original symmetry of the interior arrangement is lost, and in the last stages of its evolution the original form would not be recognisable but for the existence of the intermediate kinds.

CHAPTER III

THE NIEKERK RUINS (*continued*)—THE PLACE OF OFFERINGS

Ground eroded by rain.

IF the ruins described in the last chapter were interesting to the archæologist, another part of the same site, on which no buildings stood, was still more so. It is the first piece of ground to be traversed after descending from the nek by which the site is approached (cf. p. 14). Plate VI. *b* shows (left corner) the most southern of a pair of small kopjes that stand beside the nek referred to, exactly between the two mountains. Immediately below these, on the route towards Division VI., the ground is furrowed and eroded by the rains of many years pouring off the adjoining slopes. Within a space of about 100 metres from E. to W. may be counted five distinct torrent beds, which begin close to the kopjes and run a short course towards the valley bottom of Division VI., where all the drainage from both sides collects.

The longest of these may be traced for some 50 metres, and the most considerable has cut itself a channel of 3 metres' depth. Others are shallower and shorter.

This part of the site, which was noted as "N^K" (Niekerk Ruins—kopjes), had already been partially excavated by nature. The rush of water had washed the surface bare and cut more than one vertical section, exposing deposits of pottery and animal bones among ash heaps and cairns of piled stones. Had I needed any incentive to work there, it would have been furnished by my discovery, on the very first day, of a fine unpolished stone axe lying on the surface. The area on which I dug was not large, but probably covered the whole extent of ground in which objects were to be found. The line from E. to W. was exactly conterminous with the two kopjes and the space between them; that is to say, it measured about 110 metres long. In the N. and S. line it measured as nearly as possible the same, beginning only a few metres from the foot of the kopjes.

THE NIEKERK RUINS—THE PLACE OF OFFERINGS

The appearance of the ground when cleared of grass and undergrowth, but before any excavations had been undertaken, may be judged from the example given in Plate VII. *a*. It was covered with low hummocks of somewhat indefinite circular outline and varying in height according to the amount of erosion which had taken place at this particular spot. *Ground eroded by rain.*

The one here figured was on the side of the chief torrent, its top being about 1.50 m. above the stream bed. All loose earth had been carried away by the water, leaving exposed a heap of ashes, from which protruded large fragments of broken pots and bones of animals. The heap had been probably 2.50 m. in diameter, but the side next to the stream had been washed away and the objects carried down to a little lower than their proper level. The top also had been somewhat denuded, so that the original dimensions were difficult to gauge. On digging into it I found that there was only in reality a depth of 0.40 m. above the bed-rock at the centre. Other heaps were less well defined; often they had been denuded to the ground-level, and, unless they stood on the actual side of one of the torrents, it was necessary to dig a trench, beginning outside in a soil of flinty hardness, and to run it through them. It appears, however, that they were of very various dimensions. A diameter of 2.50 m., with a depth of 1 metre, was perhaps the most typical, but some were much larger, and some very much smaller. *Deposits of ashes, bones, and pottery.*

On the same piece of ground, but confined to the southern side of it, were scattered small cairns of stones. These I supposed at first to be superstructures erected over such deposits as have just been described. But some trial excavations disproved this very natural view. In a case where such a cairn did actually cover an ash heap, it was by no means over the centre of it, and in three other cases there was nothing whatever *beneath* the cairn. On the other hand, there were deposits close beside it. In other parts, where no traces of them remain, cairns may have been demolished by the water and scattered, but I cannot avoid the conclusion that though the two are connected by some relation, yet neither is an indispensable accompaniment to the other. So far as can be judged from the present state of the ground, the deposit heaps outnumber the cairns. The latter are rings averaging 2 m. to 2.50 m. in diameter, filled in with small unhewn stones of granite and quartz, and rising 0.30 m. to 0.40 m. above the ground. *Cairns of stones.*

The deposit heaps were composed of wood ashes, which had mixed with the earth and set so hard that it was difficult to extract the objects buried in them. Where the most perfect sections were visible it could be observed that *Remains of ceremonial feasts.*

Niekerk Ruins. The Place of Offerings.

Remains of ceremonial feasts.

originally there had been several layers of bulky jars placed one on the top of the other, and that their contents had poured out on the ground.

Whether the jars had been originally laid on a bed of ashes, or whether the deposit was formed entirely of what they had contained, was not always easy to determine. But from the size of the logs of charred wood (0.15 m. in diameter) which occurred in some of the deposits, it would seem that some preliminary burning had taken place on the spot, even before the pots were put in.

The contents, consisting mainly of broken and split animal bones, showed what the character of this burning had been. It was evidently a ceremonial feast that was celebrated here in the neighbourhood of the cairns under the shadow of the great mountain. The remains of it were gathered up and placed in the jars, which were then carefully buried in the earth.[5]

The most numerous objects recovered from the ash heaps were naturally the jars, almost all of which had been broken when originally interred. In spite of the most careful excavating, it was very difficult to get out even the sherds intact, but by very slow and laborious clearing with knives, chisels, and the pointed end of a native axe, I succeeded in recovering a considerable quantity in a fair state of preservation.

The most perfect specimens were obtained from a deposit on the side of a torrent-bed, where a completely vertical section had been exposed and much of the pottery washed half out. From this spot (N^K 17) came not only the handsomest pottery but some of the most interesting objects of other kinds, and the clearing of it showed that the only satisfactory way of working these places was to cut in vertically. For in ground of such flinty hardness the attempt to dig down in horizontal stages from the surface is bound to fail. The objects are destroyed because it is impossible to divine their form, whereas if a trench is dug outside, extending down to the bottom of the deposit, so as to lay the whole side of it bare, it is possible to clear away the rubbish gradually from between the interstices and to see the outline of the pots as they lie *in situ*.

Objects found in the deposits.

I cleared nine considerable deposits, besides digging without result under several cairns and in various places where, although sherds or objects appeared on the surface, the original heaps had been scattered. The result was to obtain a fine collection of handsome pottery and a considerable number of small objects. These were all brought to Bulawayo, where as many as possible of the fragments of pots were pieced together. A representative series of them is

THE NIEKERK RUINS—THE PLACE OF OFFERINGS

shown in Plate X., and the most characteristic patterns on the broken pieces are reproduced in Plate XI. The pottery is all made by hand, without wheel or lathe. The clay is a coarse, greyish earth, strengthened by the addition of powdered quartz, and the surface is left rough without slip or colouring. On the outside, and at the rim, the pots are ornamented with geometrical designs incised with the point while the clay was wet (Plates X. and XI.). These are executed in a bold, free style, and are usually of rectangular character, though there is one case of an excellent curved mæander. A unique fragment (not published) shows that the vase to which it belongs was made in the form of an animal, the head and eyes of which were represented by incised lines.

Objects found in the deposits.

This pottery was superior to any found in the adjoining dwellings, from which I obtained nothing better than rough, domestic vessels (Plate X. Nos. 3, 4, 6), which is indeed the usual experience when digging upon the sites of houses and towns in any part of the world. It is only in graves or places of offerings that really handsome pottery ordinarily occurs; for common household purpose less costly utensils were considered adequate.

Of objects other than pottery, the most numerous were iron implements, often much corroded. These were of exactly the same character as those found on the pit-dwellings and other habitations. Plate XII. 1-17 gives a typical series of the best specimens, some from the dwellings and some from the deposits.* Besides these there were obtained from N^K the small pottery objects figured in Plate XII. Nos. 21, 22, 23, which apparently represent the fingers of a hand, perhaps a charm against the evil eye like those found in other countries, parts of two large ivory bracelets (Plate XII. Nos. 18, 25), and an ivory cylinder decorated with concentric lines (Plate XII. No. 19), fragments of an ivory bracelet blackened by fire, a bone instrument like an awl (Plate XII. No. 27), three small ivory and one small steatite bead (all disc-shaped), and a few inches of coiled copper wire. The numerous bones and teeth were mainly those of antelopes; there were no human bones.

One of the most interesting discoveries in this part of the site was that of chipped stone implements. It has already been mentioned that quartz arrow heads were found in various parts of N. VI., but other types of worked stones occurred on N^K as well as arrow heads. None of them can be said to have come from an actual buried deposit, but two were picked up on the top surface of an ash heap. The fine celt (Plate XII. No. 36) was lying isolated on the

Stone implements.

---

* Nos. 1, 2, 3, 5, 6, 7, 9, 14, 17 are from N^K; Nos. 4, 8, 10, 13, 15, 16 are from dwellings; Nos. 11, 12 are from the pit-dwelling described in Chapter I.

Niekerk Ruins.

Stone implements.

surface, and six other specimens were found all close together within a space of a few feet on the top level of a shallow torrent bed. None of them were appreciably water worn, so that they cannot have been carried any distance; in fact, being found on exactly the same level as the ash heaps, and amongst the scattered remains of the pottery and the bones from the heaps, it is quite evident that they belong to the same period, and are not more ancient. So that we are confronted with the curious, but by no means anomalous, spectacle of a people who were perfectly familiar with metals, and possessed admirably made tools and weapons of iron, but yet retained the use of stone implements for some purposes. Flint was rarely to be obtained, so they were obliged to content themselves with less suitable materials. Thus the fine tongue-shaped implement figured in Plate XII. No. 36, is made of silicified sandstone, the others are of quartz. Few stone implements have hitherto been discovered in South Africa, but the Bulawayo Museum possesses some magnificent specimens, chiefly from the Charter district,* of which I reproduce four of the finest specimens. In later chapters there will be occasion to refer to others which I discovered on sites subsequently visited.

* They were brought in by Mr. W. H. Kenny, who states that they were not to be localised in any one particular spot, but occurred over an area of about seven miles. They were picked up on the surface, and were not definitely connected with ruins, old minings, or Bushman drawings. The materials of which they are made are abundant in the neighbourhood, and according to Mr. F. P. Mennell, curator of the museum, comprise quartz, agate, chert, silicified sandstone, banded ironstone of the jaspery variety, and epidiorite.

Of the four implements figured in Plate XII. c, Nos. 2, 3, 4 are from the Charter district, and made respectively of hard sandstone, chert, and silicified sandstone; No. 1 is from near the Victoria Falls, and made of chert.

PLATE VI.

(*a*) VIEW OF NIEKERK RUINS.

(*b*) VIEW OF NIEKERK RUINS.

See pages 14, 23, 24.

PLATE VII.

A PLACE OF OFFERINGS, NIEKERK RUINS. *See page* 31.

VIEW OF NIEKERK RUINS. *See page* 23.

PLATE VIII.

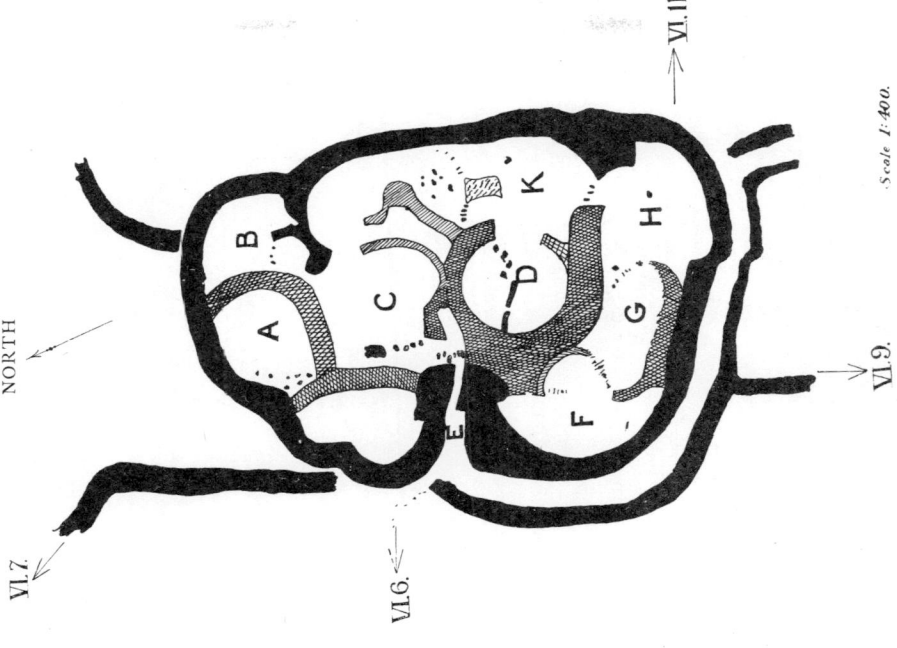

PLAN OF A BUILDING (N. VI. 10) ON THE NIEKERK RUINS.

See page 21.

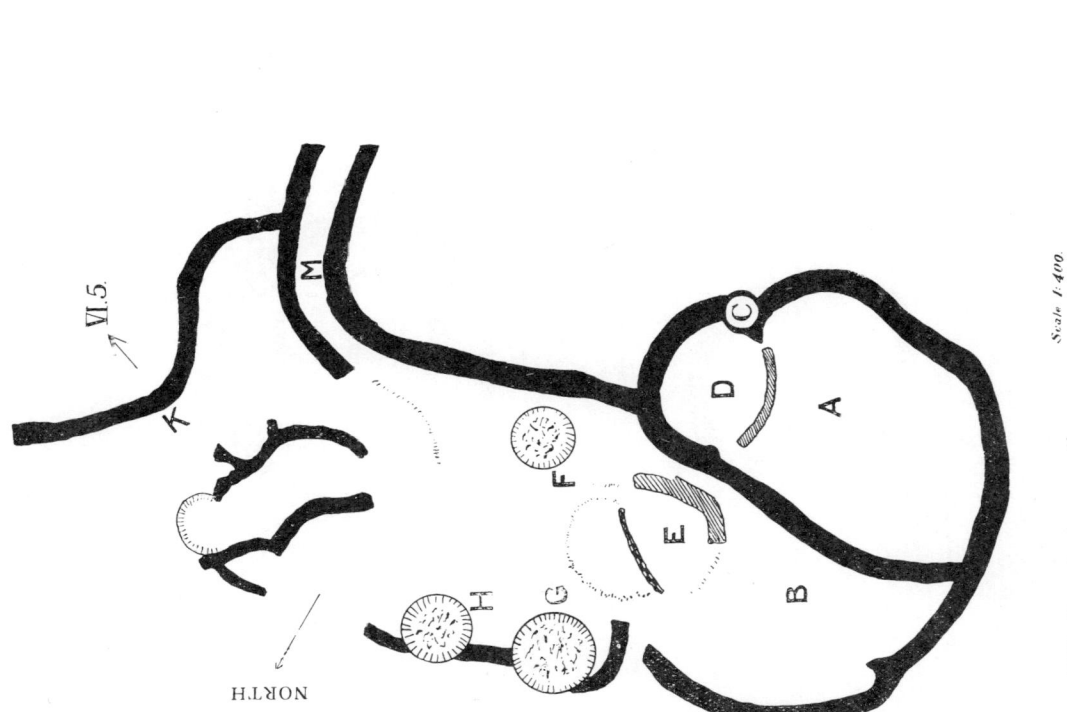

PLAN OF A BUILDING (N. VI. 4) ON THE NIEKERK RUINS.

See page 19.

PLATE IX.

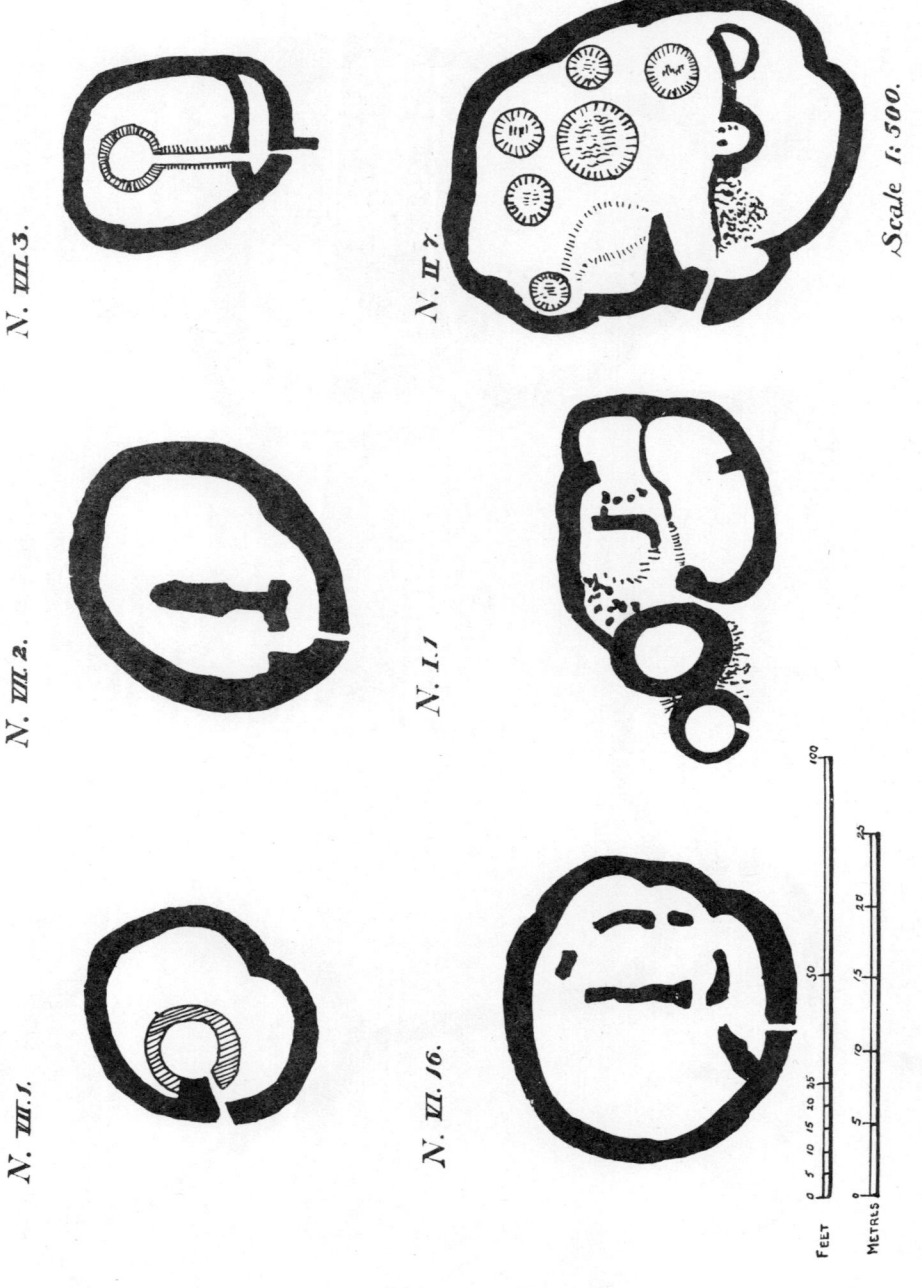

PLANS OF VARIOUS TYPES OF BUILDINGS IN NIEKERK RUINS.

PLATE X.

POTTERY FROM THE NIEKERK RUINS.

See pages 32, 33.

POTTERY FROM THE NIEKERK RUINS.

See pages 32, 33.

PLATE XI.

POTTERY FROM THE NIEKERK RUINS.

See pages 32, 33.

PLATE XII.

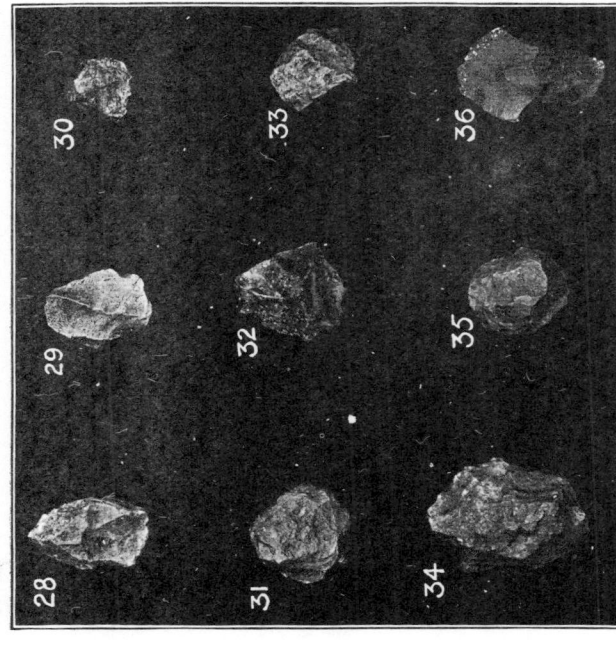

OBJECTS FROM THE OFFERING-PLACE ON THE NIEKERK RUINS. *See page 33.*

STONE IMPLEMENTS FROM THE NIEKERK RUINS. *See page 33.*

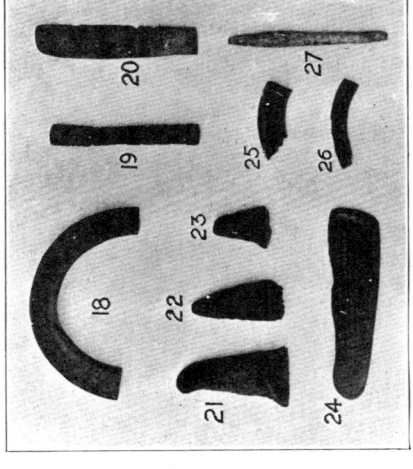

STONE IMPLEMENTS FROM THE CHARTER DISTRICT *See page 34.*

IRON OBJECTS FROM INYANGA AND THE NIEKERK RUINS. *See pages 10, 33.*

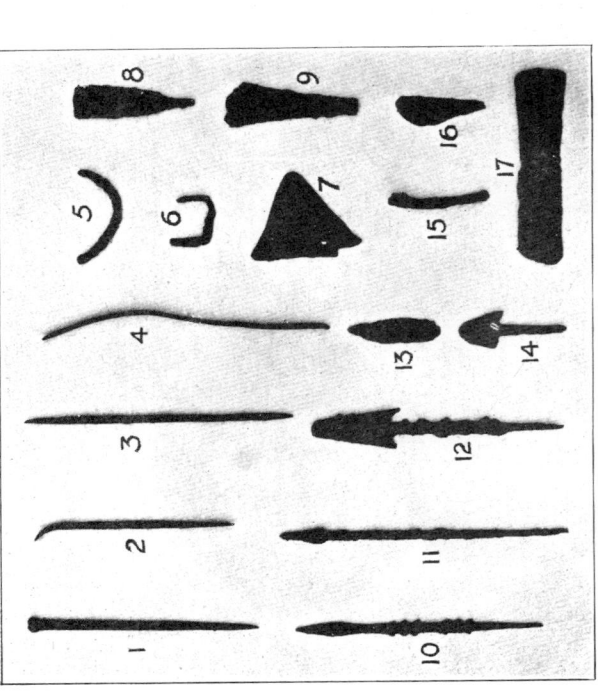

STONE IMPLEMENTS FROM THE DÉBRIS HEAP AT DHLO-DHLO. *See page 45.*

PLATE XIII.

FORT IN DIVISION II. NIEKERK RUINS.   FORT IN DIVISION I. NIEKERK RUINS.

 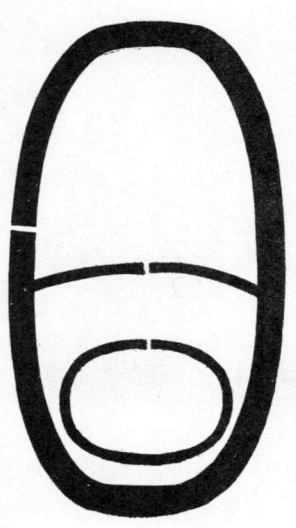

DIAGRAMS OF TWO FORTS ON THE NIEKERK RUINS.

See page 25.

PLAN SHOWING THE CONSTRUCTION OF THE ALTAR AT UMTALI. (SCALE 1:50.)

See page 36.

CHAPTER IV

UMTALI

UMTALI, the British frontier town on the border of Portuguese East Africa, has already been mentioned in Chapter I., and I have briefly referred to the existence there of various rough stone ruins. The discovery of these is entirely due to the enthusiasm of my friend Mr. E. M. Andrews, and I am greatly indebted to him for so kindly allowing me to publish in this volume the first record of his most interesting excavations. They deserve to be more fully described than the space at my disposal allows, but as only a small part of the site has yet been touched, there will no doubt be opportunity in the future to write a more detailed account.

Umtali.

The most striking discovery which Mr. Andrews made at Umtali was that of a number of unique carvings in soapstone representing, in crudely realistic style, men and women, animals, birds, and implements. A representative, though not complete, set is figured in Plates XIV. and XV. From their smoke-grimed condition it is probable that these had been hung up for some time in their owners' huts before they were buried as votive offerings in the soil of the hillside, close to what may very possibly have been an altar. This building stood on the top of a kopje, and was superior in construction to the numerous roughly-built enclosures which cover the hills and slopes around. When first discovered, it presented the appearance of an oval heap of unhewn stones, about 7 metres long by 5 wide, but when this outer covering had been removed there appeared beneath it a well-built edifice of stones (granite, quartz, schist), which had been carefully fitted and slightly dressed. It was an irregular oblong, facing south-east, just over 3 metres long by 2.75 m. at its widest part, and 0.80 m. high, with an extension 2.25 m. long at the south-west end. The interior was pulled to pieces, in order to discover whether there was anything concealed in or beneath it, but the facing

Soapstone carvings.

Conjectural altar.

36 MEDIÆVAL RHODESIA

Umtali.

Conjectural altar.

of the wall was left untouched, and now that the filling has been replaced it looks almost as it did originally. Nothing was found in or under the building, but the interior construction was interesting. The oblong portion was divided (see plan in Plate XIII. *b*) by a wall running down the centre, and the intervals between this and the exterior walls filled with careful building; triangular stones having been used freely, so that whether, as an incident of stone-laying (the object being to fix the mass more firmly), or by design, a fairly regular chevron pattern was produced in places. The exterior walls are quite unornamented.

The soapstone carvings were found buried on the sides of the hill on which the supposed altar stood. They occurred on the north, north-east, and west slopes, but not on the south. The depth at which they were found was that of bed-rock, which varies from 0.30 m. to 1.30 m. below the soil on the surface. These carvings are of the very greatest interest; the style of work is, of course, quite African.

Numerous iron implements were found in the same parts of the hillside. They are figured in Plate XIV. *c* and *e*.*

Bangles of copper wire, solid copper bangles, pieces of copper wire, and of iron wire, some pottery figures of animals, fragments of pottery, and a fragment of stoneware with sea-green glaze were also found near the supposed altar.†

Worked boulders.

If it is the discovery of the unique carvings in the neighbourhood of the altar which lends a peculiar interest to Umtali, yet the other remains on the site are well worthy of notice. In several places there were boulders on which naturalistic emblems had been carved, and rude markings had been scratched; though, of course, neither here nor anywhere else in Rhodesia has anything of the nature of an inscription been found. Some of the stones have been worked into a rectangular series of holes, evidently for playing "Fuba," a sort of hare-and-hounds, which is a well-known game amongst the natives of the present day. The majority, however, of the remains at Umtali are those of dwelling-places; enclosures surrounding hut foundations like those described at the Niekerk Ruins, in which low rings of unhewn stones have supported wooden stakes to form the side walls. The ground plans of such enclosures show a striking resemblance to those of the Inyanga district, and justify the con-

Dwelling-places.

---

* In which all, except Nos. 2, 3, 7, 8, 9, come from the neighbourhood of the altar. These others are from a dwelling-place.

† The objects from Umtali have been presented by the Rhodes Trustees to the British Museum.

UMTALI

clusion that they too are ultimately derived from the pit-dwelling. But at Umtali there are no pit-dwellings, just as there are no defensive lines on the hills. It may be of some importance, therefore, to note the gradual progression and disappearance of this type of building. At Umtali no fortification of any kind is found, and the dwellings are not of the miniature citadel type, though the resemblance of plan shows they have been derived from it. But some three miles north of Penhalonga the sides of pit-dwellings begin and extend, I believe, with but little interruption, to Nani. It is not, however, so far as my knowledge goes, until near Inyanga that hill-forts are found *as well as* pit-dwellings, and the system of intrenching great areas commences only at the Niekerk Ruins, sixteen miles farther on. From that point, however, almost every hill seems to have been intrenched as far as Nani, and there, as I am told, the system ceases.

Meaning of the seriation of buildings from the Zambesi southwards.

So that there seems to be a regular progression. The northern region nearest to the Zambesi is fortified with the most extraordinary minuteness. A little farther south, at Inyanga, the rigour of the defensive scheme is a little relaxed; then, at Umtali, the need for fortification seems to have been no longer felt. So that it looks as if the enemy against whom these people were defending themselves was in the north, not in the east or south, and the distribution of their buildings suggests the probability that they themselves first settled in the north, and only later extended their range down to Umtali.

That they were native Africans who built these ruins is abundantly evident. Their huts were just such huts as African natives use to-day; their implements and weapons, their primitive art, everything is characteristically African. No single object which can be recognised as foreign, of any period, whether early or late, has been found in the Inyanga Ruins; and a chip of glazed stoneware traded there in the Middle Ages is the only foreign object that has been found at Umtali.

Native African builders.

It was, therefore, a negro or negroid race of African stock, coming I do not know from what quarter, but possibly from north of the Zambesi, who made these buildings in the north-east corner of Southern Rhodesia.[6] At what period I will not discuss for the moment, though in a later chapter I shall be able to advance an opinion on the subject.

CHAPTER V

DHLO–DHLO

General description. The ruins dealt with in the four preceding chapters are little known, but now I come to treat of sites which have often been made the subject of illustration and description. Dhlo-Dhlo, Nanatali, and Khami are situated a considerable distance to the south-west of Inyanga and Umtali, in the heart of Matabeleland, and within easy reach of Bulawayo. Zimbabwe, is east of these again, nearly due south of Umtali, and not far from the Portuguese border.

Dhlo-Dhlo is very accessible in these days of railways. There is a station at Insiza, which is only four hours by rail from Bulawayo, and from that place to the ruins is a walk of not more than sixteen miles.

The country is high plateau, sparsely wooded with small trees, and poorly watered in comparison with Mashonaland. The ruins, which are very picturesque and attractive, have often been visited by tourists and explorers; but the only serious study of them has been made by Mr. Franklin White, to whose courtesy I am indebted for permission to reproduce a part of his plan (Plate XVII. *b*).

Fortress character. The character of the buildings is intelligible at the first glance to any one who has studied those of the Inyanga district. Their general arrangement and the details of construction alike prove them to have been a fort, or perhaps it would be more exact to say a fortified town; of a more elaborate and perfected style, indeed, than the Inyanga forts, but otherwise resembling them in all essentials. The plan (Plate XVII. *b*) shows only the central buildings, which constitute what may be called the citadel. These stand upon the top of a slight slope, in a position that has no great strategical value since the comparatively level plateau of the neighbourhood offers no precipitous kopjes for intrenchment, such as occur everywhere about Inyanga.

PLATE XIV.

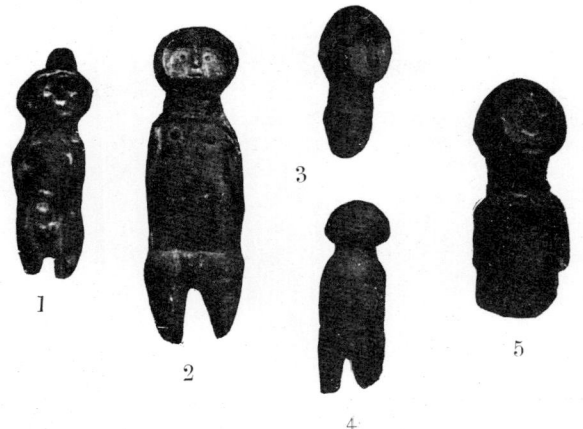

SOAPSTONE CARVINGS FROM UMTALI. *See page 35.*

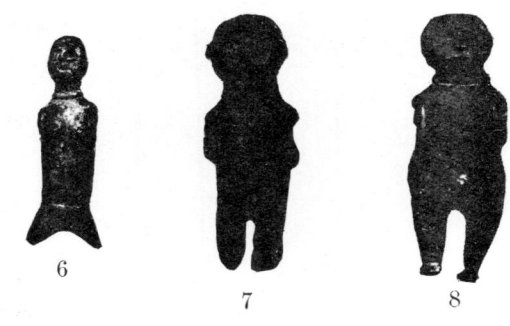

SOAPSTONE CARVINGS FROM UMTALI. *See page 35.*

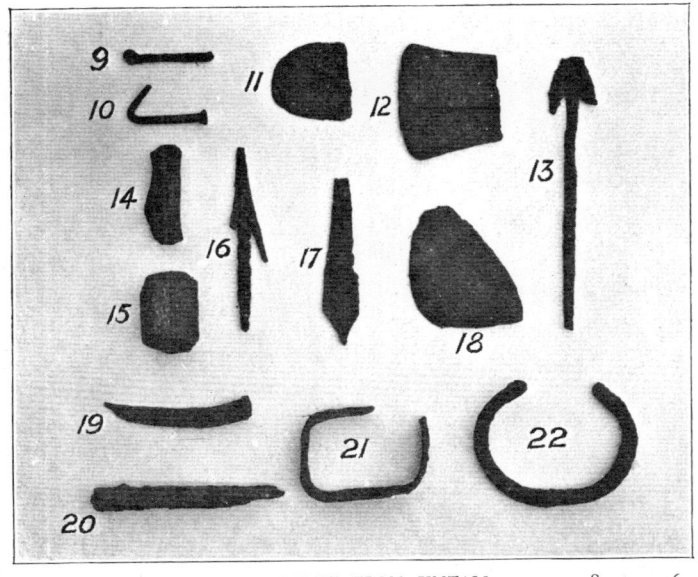

IRON OBJECTS FROM UMTALI. *See page 36.*

"FUBA" BOARD ON A BOULDER, UMTALI. *See page 36.*

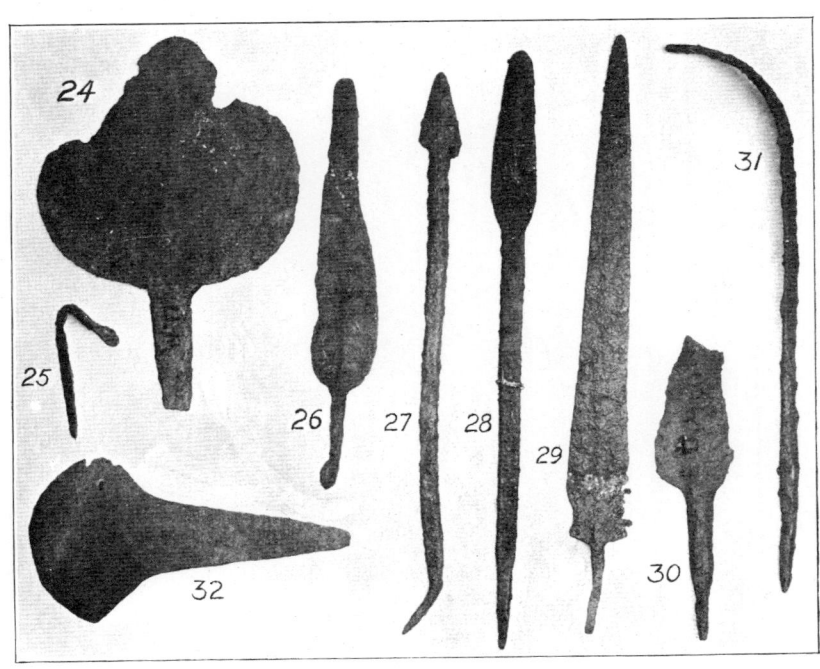

IRON OBJECTS FROM UMTALI. *See page 36.*

PLATE XV.

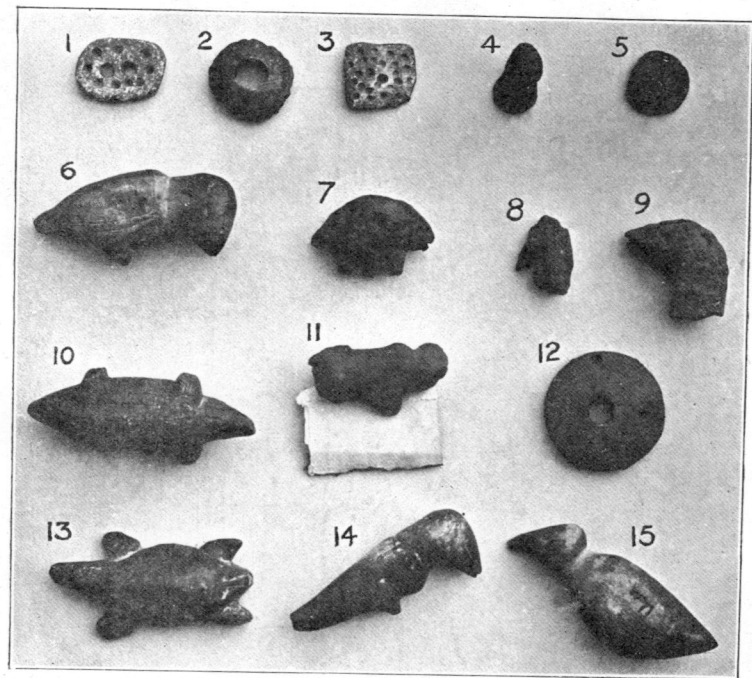

SOAPSTONE CARVINGS FROM UMTALI.

See pages 35, 36.

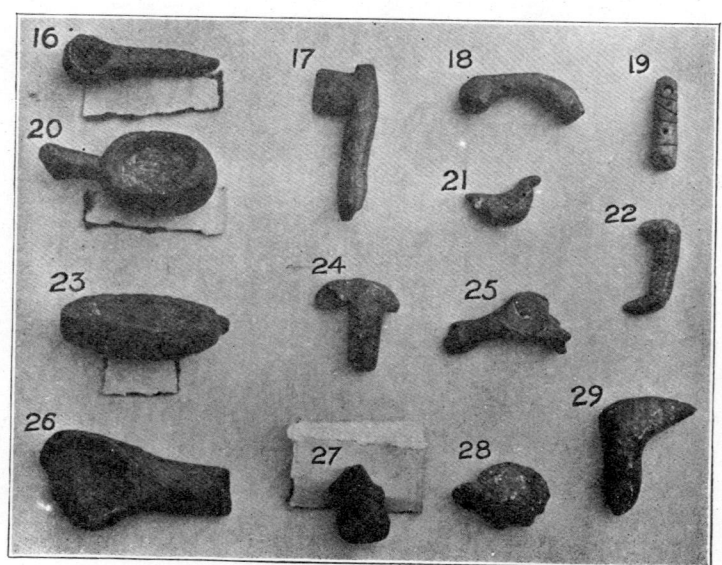

SOAPSTONE CARVINGS FROM UMTALI.

See pages 35, 36.

PLATE XVI.

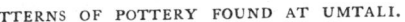
PATTERNS OF POTTERY FOUND AT UMTALI.

See page 36.

DHLO-DHLO

But the natural disadvantages of the ground have been in a great measure remedied by the resourcefulness of the builders, who have introduced a novel feature into the architecture of the citadel on its exposed northern and north-western sides. In place of a single rampart they have made a formidable front of three walls (Plate XVII. *a*), rising one behind the other in tiers. On the immediate west of the main entrance, where it is easiest to measure, the lowest tier is 0.80 m. high, the second is set back 1.50 m. from it, and rises 1.20 m. The third is 2.50 m. behind this again, and rises 1.30 m., its top being flush, with the floor of huts erected upon artificial platforms in the interior.

The exterior walls.

The defensive walls (Plate XVII. *a* and Plate XVIII.) are built of small granite slabs, very regular in size and shape, but not dressed, except in so far as the trimming of projecting ends with one or two blows may be called dressing. Mortar has been used throughout in the more carefully constructed parts. The upper tiers are ornamented with bold patterns inserted in the courses. Thus on the east of the main entrance several horizontal bands of serpentine have been introduced in the third tier, at intervals of four or five courses, in order to give diversity of colour (Plate XVIII. *a*). Immediately beyond this again (Plate XVIII. *a*) a space equivalent to two horizontal courses is occupied by a herring-bone pattern in alternate sections of serpentine and granite, with a cord-pattern above, while at the top and bottom of the wall the stones have been spaced so as to produce a chessboard motive.

On the western side of the entrance the decoration is on the central instead of the upper wall. Chessboard, cord, and herring-bone are the three patterns, the two latter separated by a horizontal band of serpentine. A little farther on, where a rectangular offset occurs (cf. plan Plate XVII. *b*), the scheme of decoration changes. The top is now occupied by a line of chevrons (Plate XVIII. *b*), below which are the cord and the chessboard. Still farther along, at the turn where the western front of the fort commences, all three tiers are decorated, viz. the uppermost with cord, chevron, and chessboard, and the two lower with cord and chessboard only. The walls of the western front are higher than those of the northern; the first is 2.10 m. high, and behind it, at a set-back of 2.70 m., the second tier rises 1.50 m. At 2.0 m. behind the second begins the third tier, rising to 1.40 m. in height.

The central part of Dhlo-Dhlo, which is all that is shown in Plate XVII. *b*, stands on higher ground than the rest, and may be regarded as the citadel proper. Its form, as usual in Rhodesian buildings, is determined chiefly by the lie of the ground, though it approaches as nearly to the orthodox irregular

The Citadel.

Dhlo-Dhlo.

Girdle-wall and outworks.

ellipse as is possible under the circumstances, the extension at the south-west corner being found necessary in order to include an outlying spur within the area of the main defences. There can be little doubt that the citadel was constructed before anything else; and possibly some of the other parts of the building which are not shown in the plan were gradually added as opportunity offered or necessity demanded. But the position and nature of these accessory parts must be understood if the real character of the fort is to be appreciated. The most important is a girdle-wall which surrounds the greater part of the citadel. Beginning at the north-east corner, it is continued all round the southern side, at a distance from the "outer wall," varying from 35 to 90 metres, and ends at that point on the western face where the single rampart is replaced by the three tiers. From here onwards the frontage covered by the decorated façade of Mr. Franklin White's "keep," by the "main entrance," and by the "approach to the main entrance," is unprotected by ring-wall; but a large irregular enclosure has been thrown out on the western side of the "keep"; and there are two smaller elliptical enclosures (of about 25 metres in greatest diameter) some 20 metres north of the main entrance, as well as a partially ruined outwork on a rock 50 or 60 metres to the north-west of it.

The four enclosures just enumerated are unessential to the scheme of fortification, but the girdle-wall is an indispensable part of it, and must have been added as soon as possible after the completion of the citadel. In connection with the tiered walls of the front, it forms an almost continuous line of defence on the lower ground round the citadel, which occupies the higher level. And where this line is more or less broken at the north-east, the two small elliptical enclosures outside the front take the place of the girdle-wall, completing the arrangement so harmoniously that it is improbable that they are appreciably later in date. On the other hand, the ruined outwork on the north-west, and the large enclosure on the west of the "keep," may well be the latest parts in the settlement.

Resemblance to forts at Inyanga.

Viewed thus as a whole, Dhlo-Dhlo strongly recalls in its general idea the large Eastern Fort at Inyanga. If the decoration, the terracing, and the careful masonry work of the central portion tempt one at first to put into a different category, yet this inclination is corrected by an examination of the other parts of the building. For, as I shall have occasion to remark again later when writing of Zimbabwe, it is evident that the old builders lavished all their skill upon the fronts and the more conspicuous walls, without ever wasting an unnecessary moment upon the subordinate parts. So that at Dhlo-Dhlo the girdle-wall and the numerous unimportant enclosures and rings against the inside of it are quite undistinguishable in style from the rough buildings of Inyanga, of the Niekerk Ruins, and Umtali. They are made in precisely the same way, of undressed and often carelessly selected stones, and might be taken at first sight for the work of some other race than that which built the citadel. And yet they undoubtedly form part of the scheme of fortification, must therefore have been constructed little, if at all, later than the well-built central portion, and contain exactly the same cement platforms that are found within it. In brief, therefore, Dhlo-Dhlo, though no doubt more attractive because more sumptuous, differs in no really essential point from the rough forts of the more northern districts. In minor details there are of course certain differences which will be noted incidentally in the following account of the citadel.

_{Resemblance to forts at Inyanga.}

Where the plan shows "approach to the main entrance" there is a sort of ramp formed by the second tier of wall, which leads up through a second gap in the wall, 3.40 m. wide, direct to a platform immediately within the main entrance, and on its east side. The relation of this ramp to the corridor or passage down the centre of the citadel is a little obscure. For, as seen at present, it blocks the passage with a heap of rubble, cement, and granite, up to almost the top level of the wall. And yet the passage would seem to be the main artery of the building.

_{The main entrance.}

However, the same peculiar feature recurs in the main entrance at Nanatali, so that it can hardly be due to any modification of the original design. Possibly the idea may have been to have the most accessible approach to the interior so far barricaded that in case of emergency it could quickly be secured. In the sides of the entrance-gap, and of the passage beyond it, several large wooden baulks have been built vertically into the masonry, and remain in excellent preservation though not sheltered from exposure. They average 0.15 m. to 0.27 m., and were doubtless intended to buttress up the walls. Unlike the entrance to the forts at Inyanga and Niekerk Ruins, this appears to have been open at the top and not lintelled with stone.

On either side of the passage, and in several other places, "platforms" are marked in the plan. As a matter of fact many more of these might have been inserted, though it would have been infinitely laborious, if not impossible, to give their exact relative position by surveying with an

_{Platforms.}

Dhlo-Dhlo.

Platforms.

instrument. For the entire area comprised within the citadel is occupied by artificial platforms of concrete, forming a single continuous block with several well-distinguished levels. Thus immediately inside the entrance there is one large platform on the west ("keep") and another exactly similar on the east side. Their floors are flush with the top of the third tier of the exterior wall.

Each of these extends over nearly half the area bisected by the passage in its north (N.-W.) to south (S.-E.) line. The remaining half is occupied by other platforms which are built on a lower level, sometimes as much as two metres below the first. Their meaning would have been plain even had they been less perfectly preserved. They are exactly like the circular platforms observed on the Niekerk Ruins (cf. above, p. 27), and obviously served the same purpose. The only difference is that the inhabitants of Dhlo-Dhlo employed a superior material. In place of clay they have used a hard cement (made apparently of powdered granite) similar to that which we shall find later at Nanatali, Khami, and Zimbabwe. The platforms are normally circular, but sometimes horse-shoe and wedge-shaped pieces have been inserted to fill in the intervals occurring where they abutted one on another. They were the dwelling-places and the workshops of the inhabitants of the settlement. One, which was partially excavated with results that will presently be detailed, may serve as a standard type. It stood a few metres to the east of the entrance passage, and adjoining the large platform to which the ramp leads up; it was circular, and measured 12.30 m. in diameter. A trench 1.50 m. wide, driven through it from N. to S., showed that a foundation of large granite stones and earth had first been laid on the bed-rock, and on this had been plastered a flooring of granite cement 0.40 m. in thickness.

Huts on the platforms.

Vertical walls of the same material were erected upon the cement floor, so as to divide it into compartments. Thus the southern surface of the platform was partitioned off so as to make an inner hut 4.80 m. in diameter, and this hut was again bisected by a wall (N. and S.) across it. At Nanatali we shall find a more perfect example, in which the central hut is like the hub of a wheel, with side walls radiating out from it like spokes to the edge of the platform.

The cement walls, like the remains of the clay walls on the Niekerk Ruins (p. 27), bore the plain impress of the stakes (four or five centimetres in diameter) and of the wattle work which had once stood against them.

The cement of the platform had been strengthened and held in place while drying by wooden posts, of which traces were found in driving the section.

Objects of great interest and importance were disinterred in the course of driving this trench. The identification letters of these specimens are "D*m*."* All, without exception, were found below the unbroken cement floor. They comprised (Plate XIX. Nos. 1-12) bangles of solid copper, and of coiled copper wire studded with beads, and a spindle-whorl. Also (Plate XIX. Nos. 13-41) a set of iron weapons found all together in a sheaf, and a circular piece of copper from the crucible, which is not quite finished, but still contains much slag. Also (not illustrated) the bowl of an iron spoon, several fragments of fused glass, several fragments of tin, ivory, beads, and glazed beads, both plain and coloured. And (Plate XXX. No. 20) most important of all, as giving an indisputable criterion of date, two large fragments of *Nankin china*.

<small>Objects found in excavating under a hut.</small>

I excavated two other platforms. They were outside the citadel, between the western of the two small enclosures on its north front and the ruined outwork. The first of these was 11.0 m. in diameter; its hut walls were ruined, though a few traces of them remained. The foundation was rubble, and the floor cement as before. At various intervals in the rubble occurred wooden posts. Digging in from the eastern side I found at a distance of 2.50 m. from the edge the remains of what appeared to be a pipe on the floor level, it continued for 3.0 m. more in the same direction.

<small>A smelting-place.</small>

Below the floor at the same point (2.50 m. from the edge) was a heap of ashes, and it seemed a natural inference that a furnace had stood there, and that this was a smelting-place, especially as several pieces of tin slag were found there. The only other things from this platform were one or two iron objects, but outside, on its north-west side, was found a piece of a four-sided slate slab, measuring at present 1.50 m. × 0.15 m. It may once have stood upright as a monolith.

The third platform was constructed in exactly the same way as the others, of cement laid upon a rubble foundation, strengthened with posts at frequent intervals. No objects were found actually within it, but the shallow layer of debris which had been thrown out from it contained various fragments of iron, an iron axe, sherds of rough pottery (both ornamented and unornamented), fragments of green glass, and fragments of Nankin china (Plate XXX. Nos. 11, 12, 16). The identification letters for objects* on this platform are D*a*, and for those upon the second platform D*b*.

* The objects are in the Bulawayo Museum marked with these letters.

Dhlo-Dhlo.

Before leaving the subject of platforms I should remark that some of them were used not for actual dwellings, but to support grain shelters, the latter being oval cement receptacles, measuring 0·80 m. × 0.70 m., close beside which there are generally grinding stones.

The great kitchen midden. Description.

The most considerable find of antiquities was made, however, not in any of the huts, but in a large debris heap on the west of the citadel ("large ash heap" in plan). Here at an angle between the walls there is a steep slope over which the inhabitants of the numerous dwellings on the citadel must have shot all their rubbish, so that the entire out-throwings of a considerable village are collected at this single point.

The heap measured about 50 metres in maximum length by 20 metres in maximum breadth; the height varied greatly in different parts according to the slope of the rock. I cut into this heap from the southern and the western sides, and found it to consist of the contents of wood fires, among which were a quantity of implements, ornaments, weapons, pottery, etc.

Most of the things were in a fragmentary condition, the pottery all in scattered sherds, and, except for unbreakable metal objects, very little was recovered intact. There was no trace of any order or arrangement, and it is evident this was not any sort of offering-place like that in the Niekerk Ruins, but merely the great kitchen midden of the town.

As the excavation progressed it was discovered that the heap was stratified in a curious way. At different levels there were thin layers of cement running through the beds of ashes. At first I thought these might have been the floors of huts, but soon found that view to be untenable, for there were no traces of any rubble foundations, posts, or walls, and the cement layers curved over in such a way that they could never have served as floors in the dwellings of people who were so careful to lay their floors truly horizontal. The true explanation, no doubt, is that from time to time the accumulation of loose stuff on the slope below the citadel threatened to become a nuisance, shifting and blowing about in the wind.

When this happened the old inhabitants fixed it firmly by placing a coating of cement over it, and thus obtained a new surface, on which they then began to throw their rubbish again. The process was repeated several times, and from the technical excavator's point of view it was most interesting to study, for the cement naturally followed the slope of the rubbish heap, and consequently flowed in curves instead of horizontal courses, as it would have done on an artificially-levelled surface. So that had I recorded my results simply in measurements, and supposed these measurements to be interchangeable all over the mound, I should have obtained quite untrustworthy results. For near the edge of the mound the cement layers were only a few centimetres apart, whereas, nearer the middle there was an interval of about a metre between them, the rubbish naturally settling more thickly near the dwellings than farther away. What I did, therefore, was to judge the levels entirely by these cement layers and to keep the contents apart for comparison.

The great kitchen midden. Description.

The principal excavation was made on the southern slope. Here, at a depth of 1.50 m. from the middle of the mound, there was a thin layer of cement, and about a metre below this (though much less at the outside edge) was a second similar layer. At about another metre lower again there was a third layer, below which I sunk one metre more, and had then nearly, but not quite, reached bed-rock. Having no more time to spend upon the site I was obliged to stop excavating at this depth, viz. 4 metres below the surface, but as no distinction whatsoever could be observed in the character of the deposits found in the several levels down to that point, and only a very slight depth remained below it, there can be little doubt that the results are representative.

The most typical objects found in this heap (the identification letters are *Dc*) are figured chiefly in Plate XX., and may be classified as follows :—

Objects found in the great kitchen midden.

(1) Iron implements and weapons, iron bands, and a pair of handcuffs (Plate XX. Nos. 20, 21, 22, 23, 27, 28 ; 14, 15, 17, 18 ; 19).[7]

(2) Stone implements (Plate XII. *d*), generally poorly worked, but No. 44 is a good specimen.

(3) Plain bronze wire (Plate XX. No. 13), twisted bronze wire sheathing (Plate XX. Nos. 2, 3, 4, 7, 8, 10), perhaps from scabbard.

(4) Copper bangles coiled on wire (Plate XX. No. 1), a copper ring (Plate XX. No. 5), cores of copper[8] produced in making wire (Plate XX. Nos. 24, 26).

(5) An ornamental silver pin (Plate XX. No. 9), slightly alloyed with copper, with round knobbed head surmounted by a kind of Maltese Cross.[9]

(6) A fragment, 0.025 m. long, of bangle made of twisted gold wire, alternated with enamelled bronze wire (not illustrated).

(7) Fragments of thin sheet bell-metal (83 per cent of copper, 17 per cent of tin), Plate XX. No. 11.

(8) Beads (thin, discoid in shape) of ivory and of shell, the ivory shown as Nos. 18, 19, the shell as Nos. 10, 14, in Plate XXX.

Dhlo-Dhlo.

(9) Small glaze and porcelain beads of various colours, viz. yellow green, red, light blue, dark blue, and plain white.

(10) Fragments of earthenware with a brown glaze.

Objects found in the great kitchen midden.

(11) Fragments of Nankin china with blue patterns on white ground, a fragment of china with marbled pattern (Plate XXX. Nos. 17, 13, 15).

(12) A quantity of hand-made earthenware pottery, of two classes, the one with painted patterns (Plate XXXIII.), the other with patterns not painted but incised with the point (Plate XXXIV. *a*).[10]

The logical principles on which Rhodesian ruins may be dated.

And here, before making any other comment upon the above list, I must clear the way by a statement of the most important conclusion to which the excavations at Dhlo-Dhlo have led. What is the antiquity of these ruins? is a question which must have occurred before now to the reader of the first four chapters, a question the answer to which I have deliberately postponed. The reason for so doing will be obvious when I remind the reader that apart from what archæological research can teach us we are necessarily ignorant of the entire history of South Africa before the Middle Ages. There is no documentary evidence upon the subject, setting aside a few vague and ambiguous references, earlier than the beginning of the sixteenth century, when the Portuguese records begin. In the nature of the case, therefore, there can be no comparative scale for dating buildings or objects such as has been established for Egypt and the Mediterranean on the primary basis of inscriptions checked and guaranteed by their correspondence with literary histories.

It follows that there is only one means by which the antiquity of the Rhodesian remains can be gauged. This is by comparing them with those of other countries for which the dating is already independently established. But up to the present chapter no material for such comparison had been obtained. For the style of the buildings by itself affords no criterion. It cannot be proved to owe anything to foreign influences; all characteristics of Oriental or European architecture are entirely absent, and even were this not the case such elementary forms could never be assigned to any closely delimited period.

Little more assistance is given by the objects discovered in the excavations described in the first four chapters. That they do not belong to any exceedingly remote period might be justifiably inferred from the frequent occurrence of worked iron; which at once excludes the Stone, Copper, and Bronze Ages, and if the standard of Mediterranean chronology could be applied, would fix the earliest possible limit at about 1000 B.C., and the more probable limit at anything after 600 B.C. But if this line of argument were adopted it would always be open to the objection that the working of iron in South Africa may have been earlier than it was in the Mediterranean, a theory which it would be extremely difficult either to prove or disprove. The shapes of the tools and weapons, and the primitive technique and decoration of the pottery, are almost equally valueless as evidence. Shapes and patterns may and do survive to an almost indefinable extent, and it is common knowledge that in many parts of the world pottery is being actually manufactured at the present day which is indistinguishable from what is found on prehistoric sites of every degree of antiquity. Unless, therefore, objects are discovered in the Rhodesian ruins which are demonstrably foreign imports, and known to belong to well-defined periods in the countries of their origin, there can be no solution of the problem. And it is just because no such objects were found on the sites of Inyanga, the Niekerk Ruins, and Umtali that I have refrained so far from expressing any definite opinion upon the date of the ruins on those three sites. If the periods of other ruins in the country can be satisfactorily ascertained, then it may be possible, by establishing a relation between the different sites, to obtain an estimate of their relative periods. This aspect of the question will be dealt with in a later chapter. *[The logical principles on which Rhodesian ruins may be dated.]*

But at Dhlo-Dhlo the required factor is found. There are unmistakable foreign articles, and these of a well-known kind. For the present purpose it will be sufficient to mention one, and that is the *Porcelain*. Many of the fragments of porcelain discovered in various parts of Dhlo-Dhlo can be recognised at a glance. They are what is known as Nankin china, a definitely mediæval or even post-mediæval product. The piece figured in Plate XXX. No. 20 is of a style known to be not earlier than the sixteenth century A.D. *[The evidence by which Dhlo-Dhlo can be exactly dated.]*

Now let us recall what were the precise points in the ruins at which Nankin china was discovered. There were no less than three widely separate points, viz.—first, the debris thrown out of a platform outside the front of the citadel (p. 43); secondly, the great rubbish heap on the western side of the citadel; thirdly, a dwelling within the very heart of the citadel.

It may be granted that the first of these taken by itself might not be considered conclusive. It might be argued that, being found only just below the surface of the soil, and only *near*, not actually *in*, a dwelling, the fragments of porcelain had been dropped there at some period subsequent to the construction of the platform.

Dhlo-Dhlo.

But the second case is harder to explain away, for, as I have already stated, there is no difference in character between what comes out from the several layers of the great rubbish heap, so that any object found in it, at whatever level, must at least approximately date the entire mass.

The evidence by which Dhlo-Dhlo can be exactly dated.

The conclusive case, however, is the third. I deliberately selected this particular platform on the east side of the entrance of the citadel as being beyond all question contemporary with the first stones that were ever laid at Dhlo-Dhlo. It is an integral part of the most essential and therefore the earliest portion of the building, even supposing (what I do not for my own part believe) that any considerable time may have intervened between the erection of this and that of the outlying walls and enclosures. Indeed, I expressly chose this platform rather than one close beside it (of which the foundations were against the front wall, and the side-walls continuous in a vertical line with the front wall), in order to avoid the possibility of the question of higher or lower level being mooted. Though in reality, of course, there is not the slightest reason for supposing the platforms on higher levels to be any later.

And yet it was here, in the unbroken cement floor of a dwelling demonstrably as old as any in the whole settlement, that the Nankin china figured in Plate XXX. No. 20 was found.

Can there be any reasonable doubt after this that the date of Dhlo-Dhlo is the date of this blue and white Nankin china, that is to say, mediæval or post-mediæval?

Remarks on the metals found at Dhlo-Dhlo.

Now that the date of the Dhlo-Dhlo ruins has been ascertained, one or two discursive remarks may be made upon the various classes of objects found in them. First, then, with regard to the metals. The occurrence of silver is interesting because it has been so rarely found on Rhodesian sites. That the mediæval Kaffirs of the Monomotapan Empire knew of the existence of silver in their country is proved by the curious history of the Portuguese hunt after silver-mines from 1572 onwards through the seventeenth century. The reigning Monomotapa, or ruler of a dominion which, according to the Portuguese writers, extended when they first entered the country over the greater part of South-East Africa, ceded in the year 1607 "all the mines, silver and other metals in the whole of his empire" to the King of Portugal in return for the latter's promised aid against the Monomotapa's rebellious subjects. And for many years the Portuguese were occupied in a vain search for the silver mines which were supposed to be situated on the Zambesi in the neighbourhood of Tete. The natives showed them specimens, but either did not know of mines or would not tell them where they were situated.[11] It would be very interesting, therefore, if it could be determined whether this silver pin was of native manufacture or whether it was imported, or thirdly, whether it was manufactured locally, but from metal traded by the Portuguese. Taking into account the several indications of Portuguese influence at Dhlo-Dhlo, I am inclined to think that the last is the most probable view.

Remarks on the metals found at Dhlo-Dhlo.

A somewhat similar question arises with regard to the tin, which is also almost unknown as a product of Rhodesia. The finding of a smelting-place proves that it was worked on the spot, but was the metal imported or found in the country? Tin is mentioned as part of the cargo of a ship from Cambay in 1519 (*T.R.* i. 104).

The occurrence of bronze, again, may be connected with this subject. Copper mines are common throughout the country, but how were the Kaffirs enabled to use bronze, which is found on several widely distant sites (cf. pp. 11, 58, 79). I should suggest that the tin found at Dhlo-Dhlo was imported for the especial manufacture of bronze, which in most other cases must have been an article of barter exchanged by traders for the gold of the country.

The fragment of gold wire coiled in alternate strands with enamelled bronze is perhaps the most beautiful thing discovered on the site. It is difficult to suppose that the natives were conversant with the art of enamelling, so that this is probably an article of Oriental importation (cf. *inf.* pp. 79, 80). The iron implements and weapons were no doubt of local manufacture, iron-working being a craft well understood by the Kaffirs; many of the types are still in use. Copper-working was also an indigenous industry.[12]

The ivory and shell beads are no doubt of African origin, but not so the glazed and porcelain beads, which may well be the famous "Cambay beads" so often mentioned in the chronicles. We learn from one writer that they were "red in colour, round, and about the same size as coriander seeds," and another states that they "are made of clay of all colours, of the size of a coriander seed. They are made in India at Negapatam, whence they are brought to Mozambique, and thence they reach these negroes through the Portuguese, who exchange them for ivory." Duarte Barbosa states that the colours were "grey and purple and yellow" ("continhas pardas e roxas e amarellas"); but the red seem to have been the most popular.[13]

Beads.

The pottery of this site is peculiarly beautiful, a typical set of it is figured in Plate XXXIII.; it is all hand-made, of an earth far superior to that

Dhlo-Dhlo.

Pottery.

Portuguese cannon.

of the pottery shown in Plates X., XI. The colouring matters of the painted pottery are probably plumbago for black and hæmatite for red. Having referred to the intercourse of the inhabitants of Dhlo-Dhlo with the Portuguese, I should not omit to mention that bronze cannon were found by some of the first visitors to the site some years ago. An eye-witness states that when discovered they were lying on the main platform inside the fort. This circumstance is of course no evidence of an actual occupation of the place by the Portuguese, who were imprudent enough, as appears from the statement of a seventeenth century writer, to trade guns and even cannon to the natives. The rebel chief Chombe, who was a powerful Kaffir and vassal of the fort of Sena, resisted the Portuguese force in 1613 A.D. with "balls and arrows." He had 150 firelocks and muskets and two cannons.* The writer comments on the folly of thus supplying the natives with a better arsenal than the Portuguese commanders could sometimes boast.

* Tinha o Chombe cento e cincoenta espingardas e mosquetes e duas rouqueiras."—Antonio Bocarro in *T.R.* iii. pp. 298, 387.

PLATE XVII.

(a) VIEW OF FRONT OF DHLO-DHLO.   See page 39.

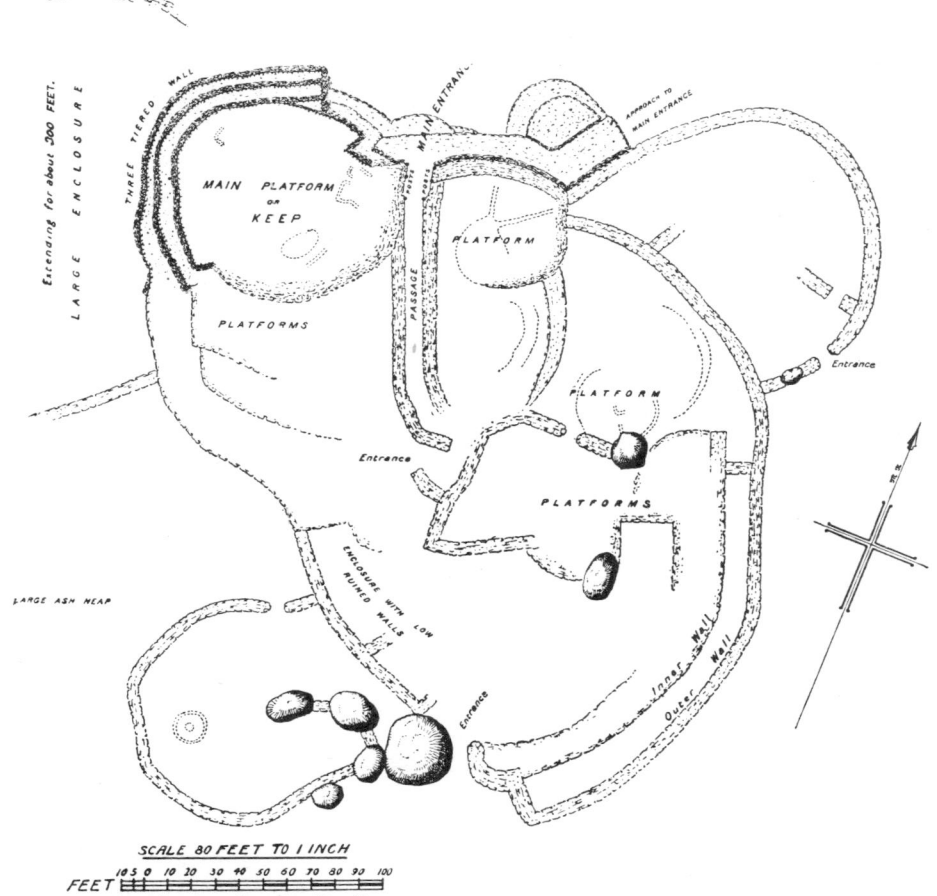

(b) SKETCH PLAN OF CENTRAL PART OF DHLO-DHLO RUINS.

See pages 39-42.

PLATE XVIII.

DECORATION ON EAST SIDE OF MAIN ENTRANCE, DHLO-DHLO.   *See page* 39.

DECORATION ON WEST SIDE OF MAIN ENTRANCE, DHLO-DHLO.   *See page* 39.

PLATE XIX.

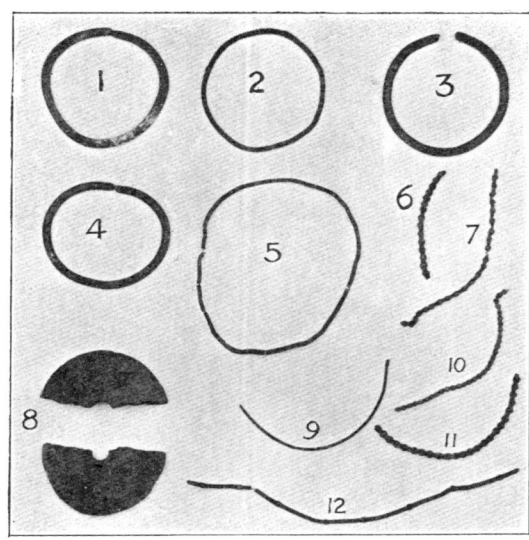
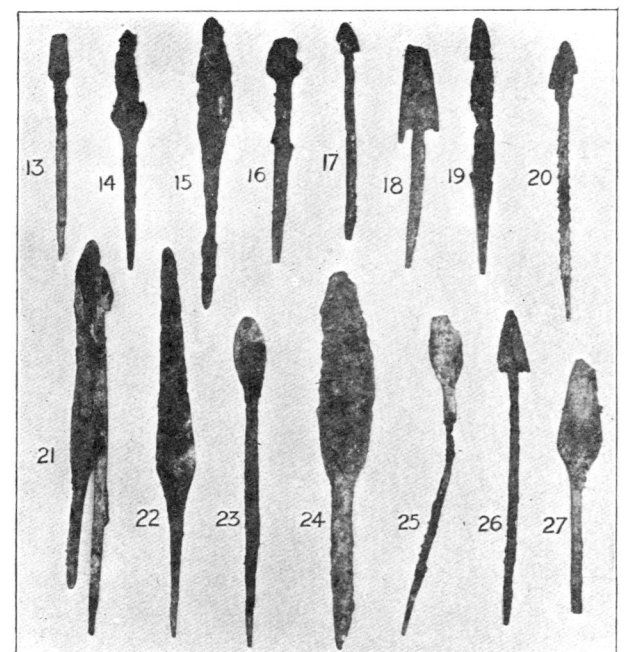
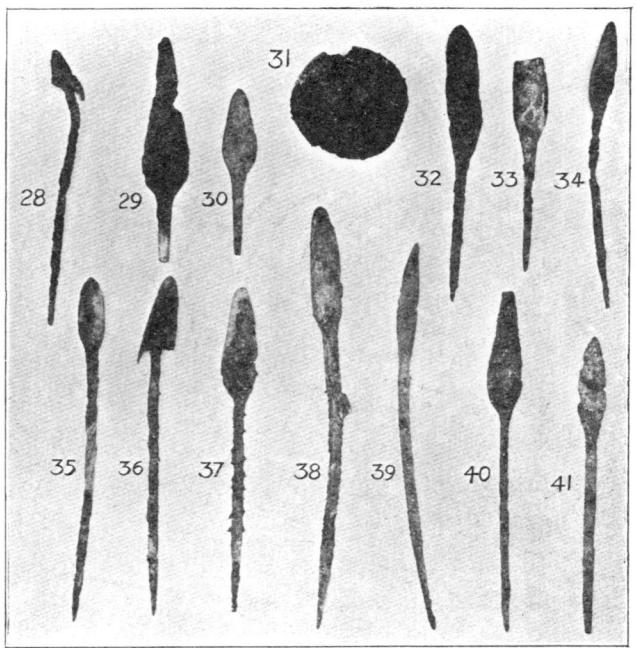

OBJECTS FOUND WITH NANKIN CHINA BENEATH FLOOR OF HUT IN CITADEL, DHLO-DHLO.

See page 43.

PLATE XX.

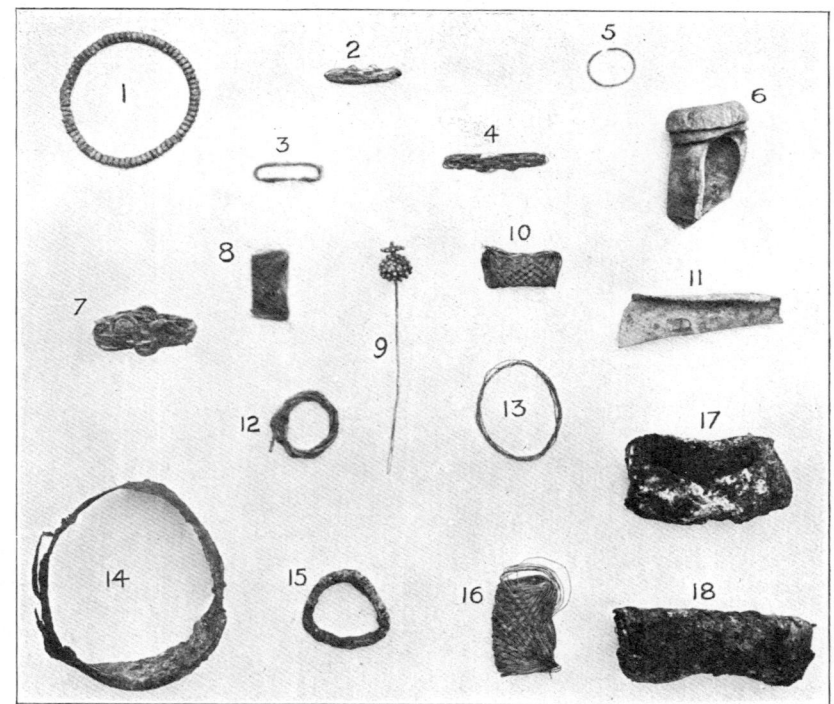

OBJECTS FOUND IN THE DÉBRIS-HEAP AT DHLO-DHLO.

See page 45.

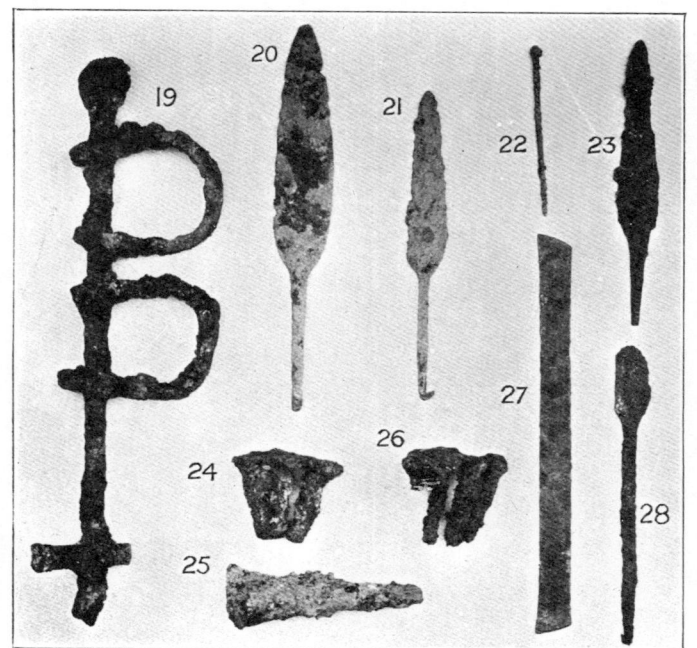

OBJECTS FOUND IN THE DÉBRIS-HEAP AT DHLO-DHLO.

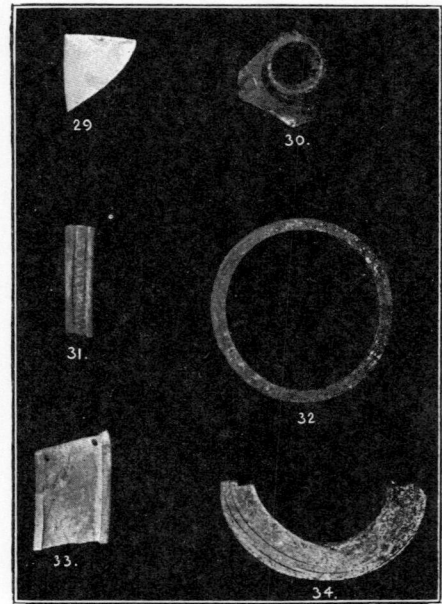

See page 45.

CHAPTER VI

NANATALI AND KHAMI

NANATALI, the beautiful little ruin of which two views are given in the frontispiece of this volume, is distant about sixteen miles to the east of Dhlo-Dhlo and fourteen south of Shangani siding. Standing on a high kopje at one of the most elevated points in Matabeleland, it commands the most marvellous view far and wide over the surrounding country. And not only its position but its architectural beauty make Nanatali the most attractive of all the Rhodesian forts described in this report. Its dimensions are small, the whole building, with the exception of three small circular platforms outside the northern front, being contained within an elliptical wall of about 53 metres' maximum interior diameter.* This wall, which on the side of the main entrance rises in tiers like that of the citadel at Dhlo-Dhlo, is delicately ornamented with the four characteristic patterns, chevron, herring-bone, chess-board, and cord (Plate XXI. *b*), and the decoration is not confined to the front, but is carried in varying degrees of elaboration round the entire enclosure. On the west side the circuit of the wall is interrupted by a large circular platform (Frontispiece *a*), reminding us of a bastion, on the summit of which are the well-preserved remains of a hut with cement walls, which will presently demand a more detailed notice. The symmetrical arrangement of the interior may be appreciated from the plan in Plate XXII., for permission to reproduce which I am again indebted to the courtesy of Mr. Franklin White and the Scientific Association of Bulawayo.

Nanatali. Exterior.

The distribution of the parts of the building centres round a hut erected upon a massive platform of cement in the northern half of the enclosure (Plate XXI. *a*). This was evidently the chief's dwelling, and is placed so high as to overlook the top of the girdle-wall. The three other dwelling-platforms

The interior.

---

* Varying in thickness between 1.70 m. and 4.0 m.

Nanatali.
The interior.

which occupy the rest of the area within this elliptical wall are built on a level about 2 metres lower, and are completely dominated by that of the chief. But the circular bastion on the west front stands on the same level as the main hut, and is connected with it by a terrace-walk along the inner side of the battlemented front wall.

From the platform of the main hut stone walls radiate out to the circumference of the enclosure, like the spokes from the hub of a wheel, and divide it into several compartments. There are passage-ways connecting these several divisions in the southern part of the building, but in the northern half the radiating walls are not pierced by any sort of doorway, and seem designed to shut off the precincts of the chief's hut from those of his dependants.

The front.

At Nanatali, just as we shall see later at Zimbabwe, the ceremonial precincts are distinguished by an elaborate decoration on the corresponding portion of the girdle-wall. From the bastion on the west front to a corresponding point on the east front the girdle-wall is tiered in terraces; and again, just as at Zimbabwe, a portion of this façade is ornamented with monoliths of stone. Two (0.50 m. high) are still standing (Frontispiece *b*), loosely bedded in cement upon the machicolated battlements. I found two others amongst the stones which had fallen from the top of the wall, and seriously debated whether I should not replace them in the places from which they had evidently not long been dislodged, but ultimately decided that such restoration-work, though it might be legitimate, was not yet necessary. It is clear, however, that each of the nine battlements, seven on the west and two on the east of the main entrance, must originally have been surmounted by these small four-sided pillars of unhewn granite.

On the inside of the battlements the façade-wall descends in four tiers to the level (2 metres lower) of the floor of the enclosure, and between the fourth and sixth battlements (counting from the west) these tiers are regularised into a staircase leading directly up to the chief's hut. On the outside the wall is composed of two tiers, the lower of which rises 1 metre from the ground-level, while (Frontispiece *a*, *b*) the second is set back 2.20 m. from it, and rises 1.70 m.; the battlements give a further height of 0.40 m. to the front. The main entrance itself presents exactly the same peculiarity that was observed at Dhlo-Dhlo, viz. that it has been blocked up with rubble, over which there is a gangway approached by two steps on the west side of the gate.

The masonry of the walls is excellent, the stones being more carefully

NANATALI

selected and fitted than at Dhlo-Dhlo. Mortar has sometimes been used, but the regularity of the facing is obtained as usual by carefully fitting the blocks and not by dressing them.

The front.

Owing to its remarkably perfect state of preservation, the fortified kraal of Nanatali—for a royal kraal it clearly is—offers the best opportunity for studying the construction of dwelling-huts and the platforms on which they are erected. We have been arriving step by step at a comprehension of these huts. At the Niekerk Ruins only the vestiges of them remained, fragments of clay, fluted with the marks of wattle, lying upon the circular bases of clay and stone which had formed their foundation. At Dhlo-Dhlo, where the more permanent material of concrete or granite cement had been employed, the walls of the huts were standing unbroken for a considerable part of their original height. But here at Nanatali the ruins are as perfect as if they had been deserted only two or three generations ago, and the cement walls of the principal dwelling-place still stand to a height of 1.70 m. from their original floor. It will be of interest, therefore, to give some details as to the construction of the two principal huts, the more so as this will explain much that has been destroyed at Zimbabwe and other places.

Dwelling-huts.

The chief's hut, which occupies the greater part of the northern half of the enclosure (as shown in the plan, Plate XXII.), stands on a massive artificial platform 2.50 m. high. This platform is constructed of large stones, kept together by several thick horizontal layers of cement, and strengthened by wooden posts inserted at irregular intervals. Its diameter is 28 metres at the bottom and 17.50 m. at the top level. The hut is a circular building, the cement wall of which is 0.40 m. thick, and still stands intact in some places to as high as 1.70 m. from the top surface of the platform. Its floor is also of cement, 0.20 m. in thickness. On the north-west side there is a doorway 1.30 m. in width, from which two curved cement steps lead down into the interior. A hole 0.20 m. in diameter on the right of the entrance may possibly have held a door-post. In the floor against the inside wall opposite to the door there is a funnel-shaped hole 1.20 m. deep and 0.50 m. wide at the top, which is sunk in the rubble foundation below the cement floor and carefully constructed of small stones. It is incorrect to describe this as a chamber, it is rather a pit, and there is no passage of any sort connecting with it. Probably it served at one time as a receptacle for valued possessions; but they had been removed, probably by the original owners.

The chief's hut—its construction.

The remaining area of the platform is divided into compartments by

Nanatali.

The chief's hut—its construction.

four cement walls radiating out from the central room to an outer cement wall which encircles the whole, so that the principal hut itself, with its central room and divisional walls running out like the spokes of a wheel to join an outer circle, is a reproduction in miniature of the plan of the entire kraal.

I drove trenches into the platform on the north and south sides in order to study the construction, and excavated the central room of the chief's hut to a depth of 2 metres below the floor, but did not find any objects whatsoever.

The second principal hut.

Next in interest to the chief's hut itself is one which was evidently closely connected with it, the hut, namely, which stands on the bastion-like platform at the west end of the front. It cannot but be significant that it is the only other dwelling in the kraal which stands on the same level as the chief's hut—the others being fully 2 metres lower,—and that it is connected with the latter by a gangway and steps. The platform is built as usual of a rubble of stones, on which a cement floor has been laid. But the hut itself presents some new features. There is a single circular room (5.0 m. in diameter) without divisional walls, and round this, at a distance of 1 metre, runs a sort of kerb of cement almost flush with the floor. It is bored with a series of holes about 0.40 m. in diameter and 1.60 m. thick, in which there were fragments of charred wood, so that posts must have stood all round to support the projecting eaves of a thatched roof exactly like that which modern natives use.

The doorway on the western side is 1.40 m. wide, and on the left (northern) side of the step by which it is entered there are two holes close to one another. These holes were filled with fragments of ivory, of which the top layer (0.30 m. in the one case and 0.05 m. in the other) had been burned. When the holes had been partially cleared it could be seen that the fragments had belonged to large elephant tusks which had been embedded to a depth of 0.65 m. below the floor, and must have stood there as ornaments or magical emblems beside the doorway.

The position of this hut in relation to the chief's dwelling, and the fact that it was decorated in this curious way, strongly suggest that it was the abode of a witch-doctor. Very possibly the chief himself exercised these functions, and if so, it must have been there that he retired to produce rain by incantations or to perform other magical rites.

Objects found. Date of Nanatali.

Only very few objects were found in the course of excavating and clearing at Nanatali, but they were diagnostic in character, and show the date to have been at least as late as that of Dhlo-Dhlo. A large iron nail, 0.30 m. long, with a screw end, was found among the debris of the fallen

KHAMI

side-walls which blocked the entrance of the witch-doctor's hut; and from various parts of the same platform came three bindings of twisted copper, two iron spear-heads, five other iron implements, and an iron band. A copper implement, two dakka pipes of soapstone, and four fragments of wheel-made pottery were found in a little debris heap outside the southern entrance.

Objects found. Date of Nanatali.

Khami is a well-known and frequently visited site about fourteen miles from Bulawayo. The ruins are scattered over a series of kopjes along the bank of a small river. It is generally reckoned that there are eleven groups, but some of them are too insignificant to be specially noticed, and I shall only refer to four in this chapter.

Khami.

The principal group (No. 1 Ruin) is that which stands on the steep cliff on the west side of the river, and is interesting as showing a utilisation of the varying levels of the ground which has not yet been met with elsewhere. It occupies three distinct plateaux, rising one behind the other in a line from south to north, each enclosed with walls, which at the present day, however, are terribly dilapidated. As usual, the shape of the enclosures is determined by the outline of the hill, but is as nearly elliptical as that will allow, the walls forming irregular arcs. It is difficult to obtain anything like exact measurements, but it may be said that, roughly, the lowest enclosure (called Platform "A" in the standard plan, viz. that by Mr. Franklin White) is about 18 metres long in the south to north line, that the central plateau (Platform "B") is 20 metres long, and the topmost (Platform "C") is 60 metres long, and that the width of each is about half its length.

Principal ruins.

These three plateaux, with their enclosing walls, constitute a fort very similar in general character to Dhlo-Dhlo, though the workmanship and the ornamentation are far inferior. The citadel, or highest plateau, is defended on the west side (on which there is no precipice to make a natural wall) by a series of ramparts a few feet apart, rising in tiers from the foot of the kopje to its summit. These are now much destroyed, but it would seem that there were originally either six or seven. In places the chessboard pattern is still visible upon them.

At the north end of this system of ramparts, that is to say, at the north-west corner of the citadel, there is an entrance passage between straight walls, approached by steps. These walls are supported, as at Dhlo-Dhlo, by vertical wooden posts. The passage, which contracts as it ascends, leads direct to a hut that stands on the highest point of the fort. It is a hut of the kind with which we are now familiar, with the usual cement floor and cement walls, and with partitions radiating out to the circumference from the central room just as at Nanatali.

On this top plateau we did no excavating, but on the next (Platform "B") we cut a section into a well-defined hut-foundation which stands there. The trench, 5.0 m. long by 1.0 deep, remains open for the inspection of visitors. It showed the usual construction, cement strengthened by vertical posts of wood. No objects were discovered except fragments of plain household pottery. The exterior wall of Platform "B" is decorated with chessboard pattern on the south side, and a little farther to the south, between it and Platform "A," there is a very perfect example of the same pattern on a piece of isolated wall.

On the third or lowest plateau the traces of huts are very indistinct, and we did no excavation there.

It is most regrettable to have to record that this, the principal and the most interesting, group of buildings at Khami is rapidly falling to the ground. Whether any steps that can now be taken will be adequate to preserve it may be doubted; and I know that it is superfluous to urge upon the Scientific Association of Bulawayo the need of watching over the ruins of which it is so proud. But it may be worth while to suggest that a constant supervision should be exercised in order to prevent trees and climbing plants from undermining and dislodging portions of the walls. Visitors also should be cautioned not to climb about the building, as every person who mounts a wall probably knocks down several square feet of it.

Between "No. 1 Ruin" and the "Precipice Ruin" is another, generally called "No. 5," standing on a slight eminence. It is in very bad condition, and has few features worthy of special remark, though there are some good examples of the chessboard pattern on the exterior wall. Within it there are cement huts of the usual type, and it should be noted that they are joined to the girdle-wall by radiating walls of stone.

The "Precipice Ruin" (No. 9) is the best preserved of any. It stands immediately above the river on the sheer cliff, and the side which is so protected needs no defensive ramparts. But on the west, where the ground is less steep, there is a finely built wall ornamented with the prevalent Khami pattern, the chessboard. A photograph (Plate XXIII. *b*), taken from a rock commanding the interior, shows the inside of this wall (centre of the picture), as well as the entrance through it at the north end. The entrance is

KHAMI

approached from below by steps cut in the rock. In the same photograph may be seen the exterior of the north wall which curves round from the entrance, and (left of the picture) a part of the interior platform, which forms the heart of the building, supported by a stone retaining-wall.

A roughly built ruin.

The most instructive part of the Precipice Ruins, however, is that which contains two very perfect huts, just north of the enclosure itself. I will therefore describe these after pausing to call attention to the photograph in Plate XXIII. a. The latter exhibits a roughly-built enclosure, the "East Ruin," about ten minutes' walk from the Precipice Ruin, and on the opposite bank of the river, viewed from a rock high above it.* It is an irregularly elliptical building, so like the forts of the Inyanga district that it might almost have been made by the same hands. And yet not only its proximity to the other ruins, but the remains of cement platforms inside prove it to have been erected by the Khami builders. This is yet another proof of the homogeneity of all the settlements in different parts of the country.

Huts at Ruin No. 9.

The same point is brought out by an examination of the two huts on a slope outside the "Precipice Ruin." One of these (that nearest to the ruin), which I will call the "southern" hut, is shown in Plate XXIV. a. Its foundations are buttressed with a retaining-wall of stone, so that as one approaches from the west, it produces exactly the same impression as the platform of a pit-dwelling viewed from the lower side. The other, or "northern hut" (Plate XXIV. b), has, instead of a stone retaining-wall, a series of cement tiers, rising behind one another to the top of the slope, where the central room stands.

Both huts have the familiar foundation of rubble and cement, and the familiar cement walls erected upon it. The walls are remarkably well preserved, and the divisions of the dwelling clearly outlined in each case. The diameter of the central room is 5.50 m. in each of the huts, and from the central room radiating walls 5.0 m. long run out to a cement ring-wall so as to divide the dwelling up into compartments (six in the southern hut) just as at Dhlo-Dhlo and at Nanatali.

We ran sections through the foundations of each hut on the eastern side, and have left them open for study. In the "southern" hut we also cleared down to bed-rock in one half of the central room, but found nothing there except fragments of plain household pottery. The posts

---

* The whole enclosure is, of course, in the same plane. It is only because the photograph is taken from above that the rear-wall appears to be on a higher level.

Khami.

Objects found at Khami.

supporting the cement are plainly visible in both trenches, as well as in the central room of the southern hut.

The objects found at Khami all came from the kitchen middens or debris heaps on the east side, and on the west side of the principal ("No. 1") ruin; the majority from the heaps outside the top platform. They comprise:

1. *Copper and bronze*—viz. copper bracelets coiled on fibre (Plate XXXII. Nos. 17, 18, 24), thin solid bracelets both of copper and of bronze (Plate XXXII. Nos. 13, 20, 25), thin copper wire in bundles (Plate XXXII. No. 23).
2. *Enamelled bronze* (cf. below, p. 79)—A pretty fragment, in which the enamelled bronze was twisted in alternate strands with plain bronze.
3. *Iron*—Numerous weapons and implements—viz. spears, arrows, axes, chisels, needles of the same kind as those figured from other sites; two unusual shapes are figured in Plate XXXII. Nos. 16, 19. Bracelets of broad iron ribbon coiled in alternate strands with narrow copper wire. A key (Plate XXXII. 15), twisted wire (Plate XXXII. 21).
4. *Tin*—A circular lump, 0.025 m. in diameter, from the crucible.
5. *Bone*—Carved amulets (Plate XXXII. Nos. 1-11).
6. *China*—A fluted blue and white fragment (from the debris heap on the east side of Platform "C" in No. 1 Ruin).
7. *Ivory*—Fragments of bracelets both plain and carved. Beads.
8. *Carved soapstone* pipes for smoking dakka.
9. *Glass Beads*.
10. *Earthenware pottery*—Hand-made, and very similar to the Dhlo pottery, both in material and pattern. Some of it was decorated with broad bands of colour—viz. black (presumably plumbago) and red (hæmatite). Some was uncoloured, and only ornamented with incised geometrical designs. In many cases the incised pattern were combined with the painted patterns (Plates XXXIV. *b*, XXXV. *a*). Also we found small pottery figures of cattle.

In various places on the surface we picked up poorly-worked stone implements. Sometimes these were on the actual floors of old huts. The great number of huts still visible, not only within the stone enclosures but outside all over the plain, shows that there was a very considerable population at Khami. The date of the settlement must be approximately the same as that of Dhlo-Dhlo, judging from the minute similarity of structural detail.

PLATE XXI.

FRONT OF NANATALI, SHOWING THE CHIEF'S HUT INSIDE.   *See page* 51.

DECORATED FAÇADE OF NANATALI.   *See page* 52.

PLATE XXII.

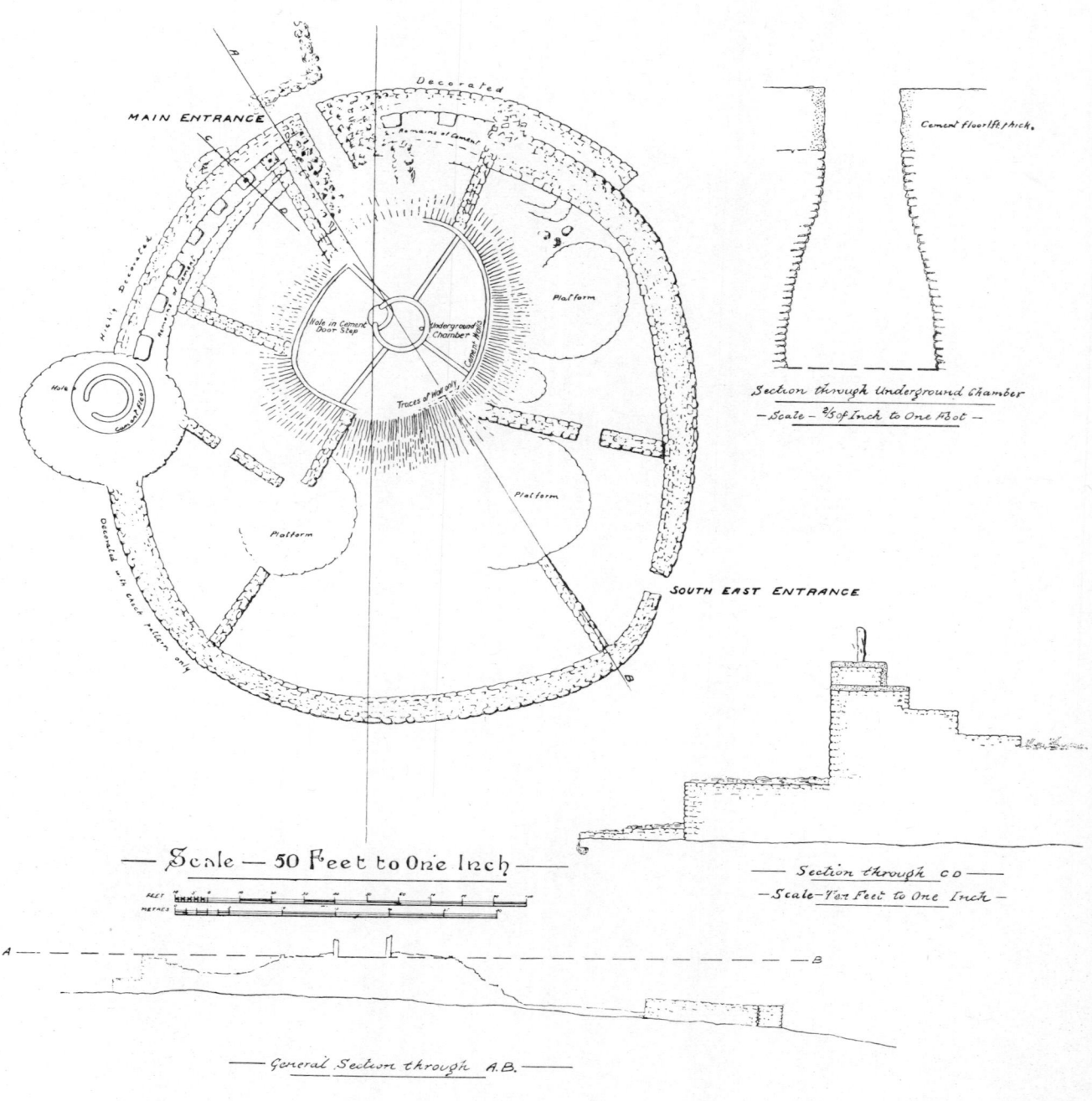

NANATALI RUINS.

See pages 51-54.

PLATE XXIII.

(*a*) EAST RUIN AT KHAMI, FROM ABOVE. *See page* 57.

(*b*) PRECIPICE RUIN, KHAMI. *See pages* 56, 57.

PLATE XXIV.

(a) HUT OUTSIDE THE PRECIPICE RUIN, KHAMI.   *See page* 57.

(b) HUT OUTSIDE THE PRECIPICE RUIN, KHAMI.   *See page* 57.

CHAPTER VII

ZIMBABWE—DATING OF THE ELLIPTICAL TEMPLE

THE ruins which have monopolised the name Zimbabwe since their re-discovery by Mauch and Bent are situated about sixteen miles from Victoria. The district is still somewhat shut off from the world, for, although it is the centre of a rich corn-growing country, the railway has not yet been extended to it; and Victoria is only to be reached by driving seventy-five miles in a mule cart from Selugwe, the nearest point on the line. *The name.*

Zimbabwe is a term compounded of two native words, and means "houses of stone." In the form "Zimbaoe," or "Simbaoe," it frequently occurs in the Portuguese records, but it would be a grave error to suppose that the sites usually referred to by that name are identical with that which is to be described in this chapter. As used by the Portuguese writers, "Zimbaoe" is merely a synonym for the principal residence of any important chief quite irrespective of locality. The place most frequently alluded to by this title is far distant from Victoria, and can be approximately located. It was in the neighbourhood of Mount Fura, and within easy reach of the Portuguese stockade-fort of Masapa, which stood on the river Mazoe, 150 miles (40 or 50 "leagues") from Tete. The Portuguese maintained a garrison at this "Zimbaoe" in the seventeenth century, when the Monomotapa, whose "empire" had shrunk to a fraction of what it had been a few generations earlier, was their nominee, if not their puppet.[14]

The records, however, indicate that considerable changes were taking place in the distribution of territory among the various Kaffir chiefs in the hinterland of the Portuguese settlements throughout the sixteenth century. And it is quite possible that the paramount lord, who was called by the dynastic name Monomotapa,[15] exercised direct or indirect control over country much farther to the south and west when Diogo de Alcaçova (1506) and Duarte Barbosa (1514) wrote their accounts than when Dos Santos (1609) published his great work *What did the Portuguese know of this Zimbabwe?*

Zimbabwe.

What did the the Portuguese know of this Zimbabwe?

on "Eastern Ethiopia." I am inclined, therefore, to identify the "Zumubany" of Alcaçova and the "City of Benamatapa," described by Barbosa with the ruins now existing near Victoria. The notes of direction and distance tally closely with what is required, the distance from Sofala being stated at twenty and odd days' march by a road which "goes from Sofala inland towards the Cape of Good Hope." *

But neither of these two authors made any allusion to the great stone buildings which have given the place its native name and which invest it with its principal interest for ourselves. Indeed, only two of all the Portuguese chroniclers have transmitted any record of them, and both accounts are evidently derived at second-hand from the same untrustworthy source, viz. the reports of the Arab intermediaries who traded to Sofala. The best known is that of De Barros (*Decades*, 1. 10. 1), written about 1552 (*T.R.* vi. 111 and vi. 267), and is worth quoting in full.

(Quotation from De Barros)—

"There are other mines in a district called Toróa, which by another name is known as the Kingdom of Butua, which is ruled by a prince called Burrom, a vassal of Benomotapa, which land adjoins that aforesaid, consisting of vast plains, and these mines are the most ancient known in the country, and they are all in the plain, in the midst of which there is a square fortress, of masonry within and without, built of stones of marvellous size, and there appears to be no mortar joining them. The wall is more than 25 spans in width, and the height is not so great considering the width.† Above the door of this edifice is an inscription which some Moorish merchants, learned men, who went thither could not read, neither could they tell what the character might be. This edifice is almost surrounded by hills, upon which are others resembling it in the fashioning of the stone and the absence of mortar, and one of them is a tower more than twelve fathoms high."

The other account, by Damião de Goes (1566), is similar in its general terms (*T.R.* iii. 129 and 55). It contains, moreover, the valuable statement that "in other districts of the said plain there are other fortresses built in the same manner *in all of which the king* (sc. of "Benomotapa") *has captains.*"[16]

It should be noted in passing that both De Barros and De Goes describe the natives of this region in their day as being negroes with woolly hair (*T.R.* iii. 129 and 55; vi. 269 and 113), and the latter states that their houses "are all

---

* "A description of the Coasts of East Africa and Malabar," by Duarte Barbosa, translated by the Hon. Henry E. J. Stanley, London (Hakluyt Society), 1866. The references to Sofala, Benamatapa, etc., are pp. 4-8 of this edition. Extracts from Duarte Barbosa are also given in *T.R.* i. 92 to 99 and 85 to 92.

† "No meio do qual está huma fortaleza quadrada, toda de canteria de dentro, e de fóra, mui bem lavrada de pedras de maravilhosa grandeza, sem apparecer cal nas juntas della, cuja parede he de mais de vinte e sinco palmos de largo, e a altura não he tão grande em respecto da largura."

ZIMBABWE—DATING OF THE ELLIPTICAL TEMPLE

built of wattles plastered with clay," adding the curious information that " in this kingdom there are no doors to the houses with the exception of those of the lords and principal persons to whom this privilege is granted by the king" (*T.R.* iii. 130 and 56).

What did the Portuguese know of this Zimbabwe?

The ruins of the *Great* Zimbabwe, as it is sometimes called to distinguish it from any others, are very imposing. They are not so extensive as those north of Inyanga, nor so beautiful as those of the Insiza district, but it is undeniable that they have a massive grandeur all their own. There are three distinct, though connected, groups of buildings, viz. the "Elliptical Temple," the "Valley Ruins," and the "Acropolis," which will be dealt with in that order.

One of my chief objects in visiting Zimbabwe was, of course, to determine its approximate date by means of trial excavations. To do this I dug in several places in the Valley Ruins and in the Elliptical Temple. The "Temple" has suffered at the hands of many excavators, and it is now exceedingly difficult to find any place at which it is possible to test for stratification of levels. One spot, however, remains. In the northern corner of Enclosure 15 a small patch of ground had partially escaped the last clearing operations, and here at the point *x*, and immediately north of it, was a fraction of cement platform which evidently still rose almost to its original height. I selected this for a test case, the more willingly as it enabled me to compare my results with those obtained by Mr. R. N. Hall in the same enclosure.

Trial section to determine the date of the Elliptical Temple.

From what was still visible there could be no doubt that close to the point *x* was the centre of one of these characteristic dwelling-platforms to which reference has already been made. Its diameter, as subsequently appeared from the foundations, was probably about 6.0 or 7.0 metres, though all the upper part, except about 2 metres on the north side, had been cut away by my predecessor. Starting in the bay made at the north-west end of Enclosure 15 by the wall of the south passage meeting that of the inner parallel passage, I first cleared down to the foundations of the south passage wall. At 4 metres south-east of the extreme end of the bay I found a roughly-laid line of stones three courses (0.40 m.) high. This line was flush with the foundations of the wall of the south passage, and ran across to that of the Inner Parallel Passage, thus barring off the corner of the enclosure. I only cleared behind it sufficiently to determine that it could not have been the foundation of an older building, but was merely the facing to a core of cement and rubble on which, probably, either steps or a horse-shoe platform had been erected. The top course was, as has been stated, flush with the

Zimbabwe.

Trial section to determine the date of the Elliptical Temple.

foundations of the south passage wall, that is to say, 2.30 m. below the top of the rounded western piece as it stands to-day, with 22 intact courses, or 0.56 m. below the top of the drain in the adjoining straight length of wall. At this level, therefore, and at this point — viz. 4.0 m. south-east of the interior corner formed by the two passages, and half-way between them, I sank a pit to bed-rock, and from it drove a trench 0.90 m. wide in a south-east direction across the whole of Enclosure 15. The granite bed-rock was found at a depth of 1.80 m. below the top of the cross-line of stones and the foundation of the southern passage-wall. Enumerating from the rock upwards there were three stratifications—viz. 0.40. m. of natural sand, followed by 0.80 m. of sand mixed with ashes,* on which was 0.60 m. of cement and rubble, finishing with a thin layer of cement. At 2.30 m. south-east of the cross-line of stones a construction, 1.90 m. high, rose above this cement floor in two tiers, the lower being 0.80 m. high, with a bevelled face of red cement, behind which, at a set-back of about 0.30 m., the second rose in a step 1.10 m. high. If, as is probable, there was any erection upon this, it had been destroyed. The interior of this construction, that is to say, the entire height of 1.90 m. from the cement floor to the top is a mass of cement, and forms in reality one indivisible whole. I must insist most strongly upon this, as Mr. R. N. Hall, who had previously made a section across same enclosure at right angles to mine, states that it exhibited "several layers of floors of a succession of occupiers each for a long period of time" (*Great Zimbabwe*, p. 263), and draws a diagram distinguishing six or seven strata above the level of the cement and rubble floor. But he is most undoubtedly in error, though the mistake is a pardonable one, considering the deceptive appearance of the section. It certainly *does* show stratification, only it is the stratification resulting from the procedure adopted in building piecemeal such a tiered platform as that which supported the chief's hut at Nanatali. However, Mr. Hall might have been saved from his very serious misconception had he observed the excavator's primary axiom and dug to bed-rock before riveting his conclusions. As it was, he stopped at the cement and rubble and did not penetrate to bed-rock by nearly 2 metres.

And yet it is only in respect of this part *below* the cement and rubble that the question of whether there was more than one occupation, or more than one period in the building can legitimately be raised. The sand immediately above the rock contained no objects, and had probably never

---

* Turned to a clayey consistency by the wet, this being the lowest corner of the Temple.

ZIMBABWE—DATING OF THE ELLIPTICAL TEMPLE

been disturbed since the day when it was formed there. But in the very bottom layer of the mixture of sand and ashes, and not only in one spot, but through the whole length of the section, numerous objects were found. And these were spindle-whorls, coils of copper wire for bracelets, and household pottery, both plain and decorated. That is to say, exactly the same objects which were found in the top surface 3.30 m. higher. The pottery from this lowest level is that which Mr. Hall calls Makalanga, and which is, in fact, exactly like modern Kaffir pottery. It occurred in the mixture of ashes and sand, not only at the north-west of the tiered construction, but at the same level exactly underneath that construction, and again to the immediate south-east of it where Mr. Hall drove his section, so that there is no possibility of its occurrence being sporadic or accidental. It cannot have come from any modern occupation since this is the lowest corner of the "Temple," and the depth at which it occurs is, if I rightly understand Mr. Hall's statement that he cleared 12 feet of rubbish out of the enclosure, fully 16 feet below the surface on which modern natives could have placed their huts. It is impossible, therefore, to resist the conclusion that the people who inhabited the "Elliptical Temple" when it was built belonged to tribes whose arts and manufactures were indistinguishable from those of the modern Makalanga.

Trial section to determine the date of the Elliptical Temple.

Conclusion that the earliest inhabitants of the Temple were some negro tribe.

This being established, the next question is, what was the earliest date? It has been stated that all the construction above the level of the cement and rubble platform is homogeneous. The date of this, then, can be fixed by any objects found within it. Mr. Hall states (*Great Zimbabwe*, p. 103) that he found in Enclosure 15 (and therefore necessarily within the same cement mass that I dug, for its foundations can be traced even now, and occupy the entire enclosure) mediæval Arabic glass and Nankin china. On his own evidence, therefore, the hut which stood in this enclosure, a thoroughly characteristic hut, such as may be seen anywhere in Zimbabwe and on various other Rhodesian sites, was built not a day before the later Middle Ages. Moreover, as this is the lowest corner of the Temple, and the foundations of all the other buildings in the Temple are above this cement and rubble foundation, it would be impossible to argue that any of them are earlier, even apart from the fact that I myself found two pieces of white porcelain in Enclosure 5, and that Mr. Hall, as I understand, found no less definitely mediæval objects in various other parts of the Temple. The date of the Elliptical Temple, then, is not earlier than the fourteenth or fifteenth century,

Period of the buildings in Elliptical Temple fixed as mediæval.

Zimbabwe.

the period of this Arabic glass, and as Nankin china is found there, it is probably even a century later, for the glass, being so beautiful and rare, might well have been kept some generations in possession.

Was there a settlement earlier than the buildings?

But was there any settlement on the site prior to the building of the Temple? The answer to this question depends on the interpretation put upon the occurrence of a layer of ashes mixed with sand below the cement and rubble foundation of the hut in Enclosure 15. As to this, I must frankly confess that I am unable to decide whether this layer is older than the hut-foundation or contemporary with it. On the one hand, it might have been deliberately placed there as a bed for the foundation; on the other hand, it might have been the kitchen midden of an earlier settlement. If, however, the latter view be adopted, it is certain firstly, that it was the same *race* which deposited the rubbish and which built the hut above it, for precisely the same objects are found within both; secondly, it is certain that the kitchen midden cannot be *very much* older than the hut since the stratum is so thin, and we have had evidence from other sites, such as Dhlo-Dhlo, of how fast such rubbish heaps accumulate.

It is so important that the reader should fully grasp the character of the huts which, to judge from still existing foundations, once occupied the greater part, if not the whole, of the "Elliptical Temple," that having given the results of the section in Enclosure 15, in so far as they decide the dating, I may now treat them from the point of view of construction.

Construction of one of the original huts in the temple.

The type of hut which must have occupied Enclosure 15 in the "Elliptical Temple" is figured in Plate XXI. *a* and XXIV. *a*, and described on pp. 42 and 53. An almost intact example may be seen at Nanatali, and there are fairly perfect remains of a good many others at Khami. It would have been a circular building with cement walls, erected upon a high artificial platform, of which the diameter at the base was 6 or 7 metres, judging from the extent of the rubble foundation at the south-east end. But as nothing is left above the foundation at this end, it is uncertain of how many tiers the platform consisted. The small fraction of it which still survives at the north-west end exhibits two tiers (Plate XXVII.*b.*), but it is doubtful whether these represent the original design of the native architect. For inside them, that is to say, within the body of the platform, is another series of steps (Plate XXVII.*a.*) that would have been indistinguishable unless the section had been very carefully dug. They are made of exactly the same cement as is used throughout, but have polished and bevelled faces. As the facing is no thicker than paper,

ZIMBABWE—DATING OF THE ELLIPTICAL TEMPLE

it is easily passed over, and any excavator who drove a trench without closely inspecting the sides of it as he progressed would cut through it in a moment and never have any idea that steps existed there at all. The base of the lowest one is at a distance of 1.30 m. from the base of the outside tier, and the whole series rises 0.90 m., after which it cannot be traced any farther, as all the upper level beyond this has been cleared away by the last excavator. The steps curved nearly at right angles across the line of my section, with the exception of one near the top, which ran in the same north-west and south-east line as the trench, though bending away from it (cf. Plate XXVII.*a*). Probably they formed a flight leading up to the door of the hut, of which no walls now remain, though I am probably doing Mr. R. N. Hall no injustice when I suggest that it was the "modern Makalanga" building that he confesses to having demolished.*

Construction of one of the original huts in the Temple.

But were the steps ever used, or were they at once obliterated by the addition of fresh vertical layers put on to form the two outside tiers? On the one hand, it is quite possible to suppose that they were a mere expedient for welding in the next block of cement, which would be quite consistent with the observed methods of the old builders.† On the other hand, it is possible that the steps were originally designed to be on the outside, but being found superfluous were afterwards walled up. Whichever be the correct explanation, it does not, of course, affect the question of horizontal stratification as dealt with in the last paragraphs. Whether the builders started from a central core and then thickened it by successive vertical, as well as horizontal, layers, or whether they worked from the beginning over the full width of their projected base, these are mere details of construction, which have nothing to do with the problem of date. However, it may not be amiss to state that the same objects were found in the vertical section within the interior set of steps as in the vertical section between them and the exterior tiers, and as outside the latter again.

While dealing with construction I should mention another interesting point, viz. that just as at Dhlo-Dhlo and Khami (cf. pp. 43, 56) wooden baulks had been planted vertically in the wet cement to hold it together. One of these, of which 0.23 m. remained intact, is shown in the plan. Opposite to it was another, of which 0.27 m. remained intact, and 1.10 m. farther (that is

---

* It should, perhaps, be noted that the natives now resident in the neighbourhood are unanimous in asserting that they never inhabited the Temple, though they stabled their cattle in one corner.

† And also of the modern natives.

66 MEDIÆVAL RHODESIA

<small>Construction of one of the original huts in the Temple.</small>

south-east) were two more, one on each side of the trench, measuring respectively 1.10 m. and 0.60 m. The top of the wooden baulk shown in the section was as high as the top of the highest remaining interior step; the tops of the other three were 0.10 m. and 0.20 m. lower; and it is certain that the longest of them, if not all, penetrated to the cement and rubble foundation, proving conclusively, if further proof were needed, the unity of the structure in which they were imbedded.

The delusive appearance of stratification in this building is to be explained by the method adopted in laying the cement. When one bed of soft cement had been laid, wood was put upon it and a fire lighted to harden it, so that distinct lines of charcoal can be seen at all depths. Thus the platform was built up piece by piece from the bottom, and perhaps at the same time widened thickness by thickness from a central core. All manner of debris that might be lying about, potsherds, pebbles, and broken stuff of every description was thrown in to make a stiffer concrete, and to this practice we owe the preservation of so much valuable dating material. Any large and complete objects that have been found below the surface were doubtless part of a foundation deposit such as was discovered (p. 43) under the floor of the platform at Dhlo-Dhlo.

This section in Enclosure 15 has not been filled in, but left open for archæologists to study. Details of other sections, which I dug in the Elliptical Temple but filled in again, are given in the Appendix.

Having determined the period at which the "Elliptical Temple" was built, I will proceed in the next chapter to describe its chief features.

CHAPTER VIII

ZIMBABWE—DESCRIPTION OF THE "ELLIPTICAL TEMPLE"

THE "Elliptical Temple" is the most famous building in Rhodesia. It owes its celebrity, as well as its name, to the late Mr. Theodore Bent, who explored it in 1891, and who describes it in his *Ruined Cities of Mashonaland*. Since that time several excavators, possessed in general of more zeal than judgment, have cleared it not only of encumbering debris but of many of its characteristic features, so that at the present day, though the visitor can walk freely about every part of it, he will not find it easy to reconstruct an imaginary picture of the interior.

The walls and enclosures, as they at present stand, have been surveyed by Mr. Franklin White, to whom and to the Scientific Society of Rhodesia I am indebted for permission to publish the plan given in Plate XXV.

The "Temple," to retain the time-honoured, though probably incorrect name, is an irregularly elliptical enclosure, of which the design is not by any means unique. It is unnecessary to fly to Arabia to find examples of a style of construction which any one who has read the preceding chapters will recognise to be thoroughly characteristic of ruins all over Rhodesia, from the rough forts and enclosures of Inyanga or the Niekerk Ruins to the beautiful little Nanatali.

It measures 292 feet* in maximum length by 220 feet in maximum breadth, and is encircled by a wall of extraordinary massiveness (Plate XXVI.*a*), which stands in places over 30 feet high, and is 14 feet wide at the broadest part of the summit. The wall is built as usual of carefully selected but not quarried granite slabs, which have been obtained from the natural flaking of the native rocks, and very roughly trimmed rather than dressed, as we understand stone-masons' dressing. Mortar has not been used, and what

---

* In this chapter I quote all measurements in feet, as I am following Mr. Franklin White. When I give my own measurements they are always on the metric scale.

Zimbabwe.

The "Elliptical Temple."

solidity the masonry possesses is due to the great breadth at the base and the care with which the courses are laid.

The breadth is always considerable, and varies greatly in different parts. The finest part of the great girdle-wall is on the eastern and southern sides, and the inferiority of construction on the west has led various observers to conjecture that the western part of the main wall had been rebuilt at a later time.

It has further been asserted in a recent work that this part of the wall differs greatly from the remainder, also that there is a joint with conspicuous misfit, and that foundations can be seen outside which would have continued the original wall on a truer curve. Some of the facts cited in favour of this view are correct, but the inference is erroneous. There is indeed a misfit at the place referred to, and the west wall *is* inferior to the best parts of the eastern and northern, but by no means to all parts. The truth is that the building, fine as it is, has been executed in exactly the same spirit as all the other "ancient monuments" in Rhodesia. Laborious care has been expended upon the most conspicuous and effective parts, but elsewhere the workmanship is slipshod. Probably several gangs were engaged on different parts of the wall at the same time, and, like clumsy engineers boring a tunnel from different ends, they failed to meet at the agreed point of junction. As for the lesser width of the western wall, that might be easily explained by supposing that the material for building was all collected at once and the better quality and the greater quantity taken for the façade and the chief entrance. A similar tailing off of the main wall has been already remarked in the descriptions of other sites (pp. 5, 6). There can be no reasonable doubt that the entire girdle-wall was planned and executed with the exact form and dimensions which it exhibits to-day, and that it has never been reconstructed in whole or in part.

An almost equally positive assertion may be made with regard to the interior of the Temple. Apart from one, or perhaps two, spots at the northwest end, where the Makalanga stabled their cattle a generation ago, and a few stones are roughly heaped without even being laid in proper courses, there are no indications of additions or rebuilding. Certain walls and parts of walls have been classed as "Makalanga," or less definitely as "ancient reconstruction," but they are more probably examples of a slovenliness which is quite characteristic of the original masons. Close examination proves them to form an essential part of the original scheme, and there is no certain evidence even of repair.

ZIMBABWE—DESCRIPTION OF THE "ELLIPTICAL TEMPLE"

The façade is decorated on the south and south-east with the famous chevron pattern (Plate XXVI. *a*), to which such exaggerated importance was attached by those who first reported on the building, as well as with monoliths, and, according to indications only recently discovered, with round towers. The chevron is finely executed in a bold style, which is better suited to the scale of the wall than the more delicate ornamentation of Dhlo-Dhlo or Nanatali would have been.

The "Temple" is evidently a fort, and may properly be regarded as an elaboration and development on a very large scale of the little strongholds built on the kopjes of Inyanga and the Niekerk Ruins. The rough fort in Division I. of the latter site (Plate XIII. *a*), with its subdivisions, its passage between girdle-wall and interior enclosure, and its dwelling-platforms, is almost a complete prototype. Indeed, the Zimbabwe Temple is mainly distinguished only by its greater dimensions and its more massive construction. Otherwise the analogy of general idea is very close, although, of course, as the royal residence and probably the original capital of the Monomotapan State, Zimbabwe parades a grandeur superior to anything that can be found among the humble inhabitants of the northern districts.

The disposition of the interior, so far as it can be judged from existing walls, is shown in Mr. Franklin White's careful plan; but so much has been destroyed by various explorers at different times that the best survey must be incomplete and inadequate for the explanation of the original arrangement. The eye, however, that has become accustomed to Rhodesian ruins by studying a representative number in different parts of the country may be able to trace the original lines of ruined walls and enclosures from slight indications which are still visible. And so, without venturing so far as to draw anything fresh upon the plan, I would suggest that there are some places where spaces might be filled and lines of walls continued with a great degree of conjectural probability.

In the first place, it does not seem to have been appreciated that almost the whole central and eastern area was occupied with cement platforms, just as at Dhlo-Dhlo and at Nanatali, where hardly a foot of space had been left vacant. I can indicate the approximate positions of at least six which are not delineated in the plan, besides the clearly-defined platform decorated with monoliths which was only recently discovered. The approximate centre of each of these is shown by the letter *x*; their diameter, except in the case of

Zimbabwe.

Enclosure 15, can only be conjectured now that so much of them has been cut away.

The "Elliptical Temple."

Starting just outside the south-west corner of Enclosure 1 there is a circle marked *M*. This should be of slightly greater diameter than it is shown, and the little wall connecting it with Enclosure 1 should be produced on the southern side. It will then meet a continuation of the wall of the west passage, which ought to sweep sharp round to the right from the broken end shown in the plan, so as to form an arc continuous with Bent's "altar"—the piece shown by dotted lines between the south passage and the letters of the word "area." The conjectural line of this wall is shown by the letters *w, w, w*. It curves into bays and does not continue as far as the southern end of the "altar," but is interrupted by a platform (*x*) which filled in the whole interval. It is pierced by two entrances—viz. one where it first turns to the east, the other a few feet west of the platform.

Bent's "altar," then, is not an isolated building but part of an enclosing wall, in the circuit of which there is a dwelling-platform interrupting the line, just as at Nanatali and elsewhere. Between my conjectural restoration of the wall and the northern doorway of Enclosure 7 a small arc is indicated, which should be restored as a circular platform (*x*) occupying the centre of the roadway. Passing eastward from here along the northern wall of Enclosure 10 a large platform, or possibly two (*x*), stood on to the north-east of Enclosure 10. There was another (*x*) in Enclosure 13, almost abutting on the lately discovered platform with the decoration of monoliths. Where an "earth bank" is marked in the middle of the east wall of 7 was evidently a large circular platform; and, finally, in 15 there was a platform (*x*), through which I drove a section that will presently be described.

One other new point has to be mentioned, which is, that in 14, where a tooth-shaped protuberance is planned against the wall of the "parallel passage," there is really a large buttress, approximately 5.50 m. long (excluding two metres of fallen stuff at the south end), which projects about 2.50 m. from the wall. A little stone staircase with rounded face ascends it, projecting 0.80 m. from the passage-wall; the upper courses of it are plainly visible, though the lower are ruined.

As thus modified, the plan of the Temple is more intelligible. It seems to fall naturally into two nearly equal divisions, a southern (south-eastern) and a northern (north-western), separated by a wide roadway across the centre of the building. The southern division would be outlined by continuing the north walls of 7 and 10 to the staircase at 14. The other division would be bounded by the conjecturally restored wall continuing the west passage (*w*, *w*, *w*) to Bent's "altar." As to Enclosure 15, I am doubtful whether it should be included in the northern division, or whether it combines with some of the ground on the east and south of it to form a third division, or yet, again, whether it was left unenclosed. However this may be, there is no doubt that both it and the roadway leading to it were occupied by cement platforms.

The northern division of the "Temple" exhibits the same scheme of arrangement as that seen in its most perfect form at Nanatali; that is to say, a central enclosure (No. 1 in this case), from which divisional walls radiate like the spokes of a wheel to the great girdle-wall. It has its proper entrance from the outside, viz. the "north-west entrance"; and, just as at Nanatali, this is shut off from the remainder of the building by the radiating walls of Enclosures 3 and 4.

Enclosure 1 is also served direct by another entrance, the "north entrance," which, however, only leads into it by a narrow, winding passage. On its south side the whole northern division would be bounded and cut off from the other part by my restored wall, which, of course, does not constitute an absolute barrier (pierced as it is by two small entrances and interrupted by a platform), but when joined on to the section of building which Bent called an "altar," makes a continuous arc such as forms the girdle-wall of the citadel at Dhlo-Dhlo and elsewhere. Between this encircling line and the southern wall of Enclosure 1 are the remains of several cement constructions.

There is the most unmistakable evidence that Enclosure No. 1 was occupied as a place of residence. Its floor is entirely covered by two or three dwelling-platforms of the usual Dhlo-Dhlo and Nanatali type, and on one of these the divan so characteristic of both ancient and modern native dwellings still stands. It exactly resembles the divan as found in the huts of the Inyanga and Niekerk Ruins, except that it is made of cement instead of clay.

According, therefore, to the theory which I would suggest, this northern division of the "Temple" was essentially the residential part, and, since Zimbabwe may very probably be identified as the old Monomotapan capital, and the Elliptical Temple is the most considerable building on the site, it is hardly too audacious to style the northern half of the "Temple" the "Royal Apartments" and the whole building, in more genuinely African terminology, *The Great Chief's Kraal*.

The southern half of the Elliptical "Temple" is less regularly laid out,

Zimbabwe.

The "Elliptical Temple."

and it is here that we are confronted with several unique features. The first point to be observed is that its interior limits are very nearly conterminous with those of the decorated façade of the exterior wall. They would, in fact, be exactly conterminous if their western boundary was placed not at Enclosure 6 but at the doorway on the west of 8. This would oblige us to regard 7 and 10 as in some way an annexe or dependency rather than an essentially constituent part of the southern division; and something might be said for this view. It should be observed that the circular platform on the east side of 7 and the famous platform in front of the cone are built in the actual line of their respective walls, a peculiarity in the methods of the Rhodesian architects which was found both at the Niekerk Ruins and at Nanatali. Moreover, that the platform of Enclosure 7 stands in much the same position relative to the cone and the platform in front of the cone as the witch-doctor's hut at Nanatali held relatively to the chief's hut there. And thirdly, that the custom of distinguishing a specially venerated precinct by a patterned façade is one that has already been observed at Nanatali. In fact, the plan of a fort in Division I. on the Niekerk Ruins (Plate XIII.*a*) combined with the essential features of a kraal of the Nanatali type, explains almost everything in the "Elliptical Temple" of Zimbabwe.

The southern division may be approached from either side, viz. by the west entrance over Enclosure 5 and the open roadway leading along the north side of Enclosure 10, or by the north ("main") entrance which leads to it by way of either the "parallel passage" or the "inner parallel passage." Probably the most orthodox way for such of the general public as might wish to come there was by the west entrance, and the other was reserved for the chief himself, and perhaps only used on solemn occasions. That the parallel passage is not unique but is found in other forts I have already shown, and need only remark here that its title is somewhat of a misnomer. For there is no such thing as another passage, in the proper sense of the word, outside the girdle-wall. What is generally styled the "outer parallel passage" is merely the space left between the girdle-wall of the "Temple" and another series of independent buildings erected just outside it. The "outer parallel passage" is no more to be regarded as a dromos or avenue of approach than the "north-east passage." For the latter is a mere alley made almost fortuitously by the walls of two buildings which would abut on one another but that for convenience a space has been left between them through which a man can just squeeze.

It should be remarked in passing that photographs of the "parallel

ZIMBABWE—DESCRIPTION OF THE "ELLIPTICAL TEMPLE"

passage" are generally misleading, as they represent the inner wall to be too high; it is really only half the height of the main or girdle-wall.

The "Elliptical Temple."

The passage, then, and the decorated façade can be matched from other sites, but there is one unique feature in the southern half of the Elliptical Temple, and that is the famous cone, or conical tower, with the lesser cone beside it. Small cylindrical erections occur in other parts of Zimbabwe, viz. in the Valley Ruins, but do not seem to be of the same character as that in the "Elliptical Temple." From its peculiar position in relation to other parts of the building, it is almost impossible to avoid the conclusion that this had some symbolical or ceremonial meaning. The problem, however, is rendered more complex by the existence of a second minor cone, or rather, perhaps, it should be said of a second cylindrical tower, for the conical form is probably only the result of the exigencies of building which required a severe batter in a building of such height.

It is moreover asserted, on the authority of one of the original gold-hunters who ransacked this site, that yet another minor cone or cylinder once stood on the other side of the large one. In any case, however, the great cone is a unique feature in Rhodesian ruins, and I am inclined to think that in this very fact lies the explanation of its meaning. The ordinary interpretation which would make it the embodiment of Phallic Worship is, to say the least, exceedingly rash. For it is necessary to distinguish between ceremonies and worship, between charms and idols. No one denies that phallic emblems have been unearthed at Zimbabwe, but so have many other objects which it is not suggested were ever worshipped. That these negroes, like all other negroes, revelled in obscenity is probable enough. That they had orgiastic rites, like every other primitive people, from China to Peru, we may well believe. And the phallic emblems may well be charms connected with such rites. But it would be difficult to produce well authenticated evidence of such a *worship* as it has been suggested that the great cone represents.[17]

Again, Zimbabwe is by no means the only place where phalli have been discovered; they have been found at Umtali and at Khami, and no doubt elsewhere. Yet it is only at Zimbabwe that a great tower exists; and this fact suggests an explanation which, though there may not be an exact parallel for it, is yet in perfect consonance with African custom. The great cone, standing here in the most venerated precinct of the great chief's kraal, in the heart of his capital, probably represented the majesty of the chief himself; the lesser cone symbolised his principal wife, his heir-apparent, or his first minister.

Zimbabwe.

The "Elliptical Temple."

The great cone measures about 56 feet in circumference at the base, and its height was originally about the same as that of the girdle-wall at the same place. A dentelle pattern, now considerably ruined, ran round the top of it. The smaller cone is $6\frac{1}{2}$ feet high where least ruined and $21\frac{1}{2}$ feet in circumference. On the north side of these stands that platform to which so much attention has been devoted. So far as mere construction is concerned, there is nothing to differentiate it particularly from any of the numerous other platforms with which the "temple" was once filled. In spite of dilapidation, it can be seen that it was built of rubble and cement, and probably approached by one or two wide steps. Like so many of the other platforms, it stands in the actual line of a wall. On the east of it a narrow passage leads from the 8th to the 11th enclosure.

What gives its importance to this platform, however, is its significant position. It stands immediately in front of the cone, in the most conspicuous part of the southern division of the building, and commanding a view right across it. Near it on the west is that platform which is conjectured to have supported a witch-doctor's hut, and not far to the north stands the recently discovered platform decorated with monoliths. It has, too, its own private approach, viz. the parallel passage.

Taking all these circumstances into consideration, I think that the suggestion made by previous writers is correct, and that this platform was a sort of dais or pulpit where a priest or king officiated, or from which he addressed an audience. I would go further and suggest that the whole southern division of the "Elliptical Temple" was devoted to ceremonial, perhaps to religious uses. The "platform area" on this supposition would be a sort of hall of audience, the platform itself a dais or throne for the king. Enclosure 11 may well have been reserved for priests or indunas, distinguished as it is by a special colour decoration of ironstone inserted in the wall. In front of the throne and the nobles stood the platform decorated with monoliths; behind them the symbol of the chief's majesty, the great conical tower.

PLATE XXV.

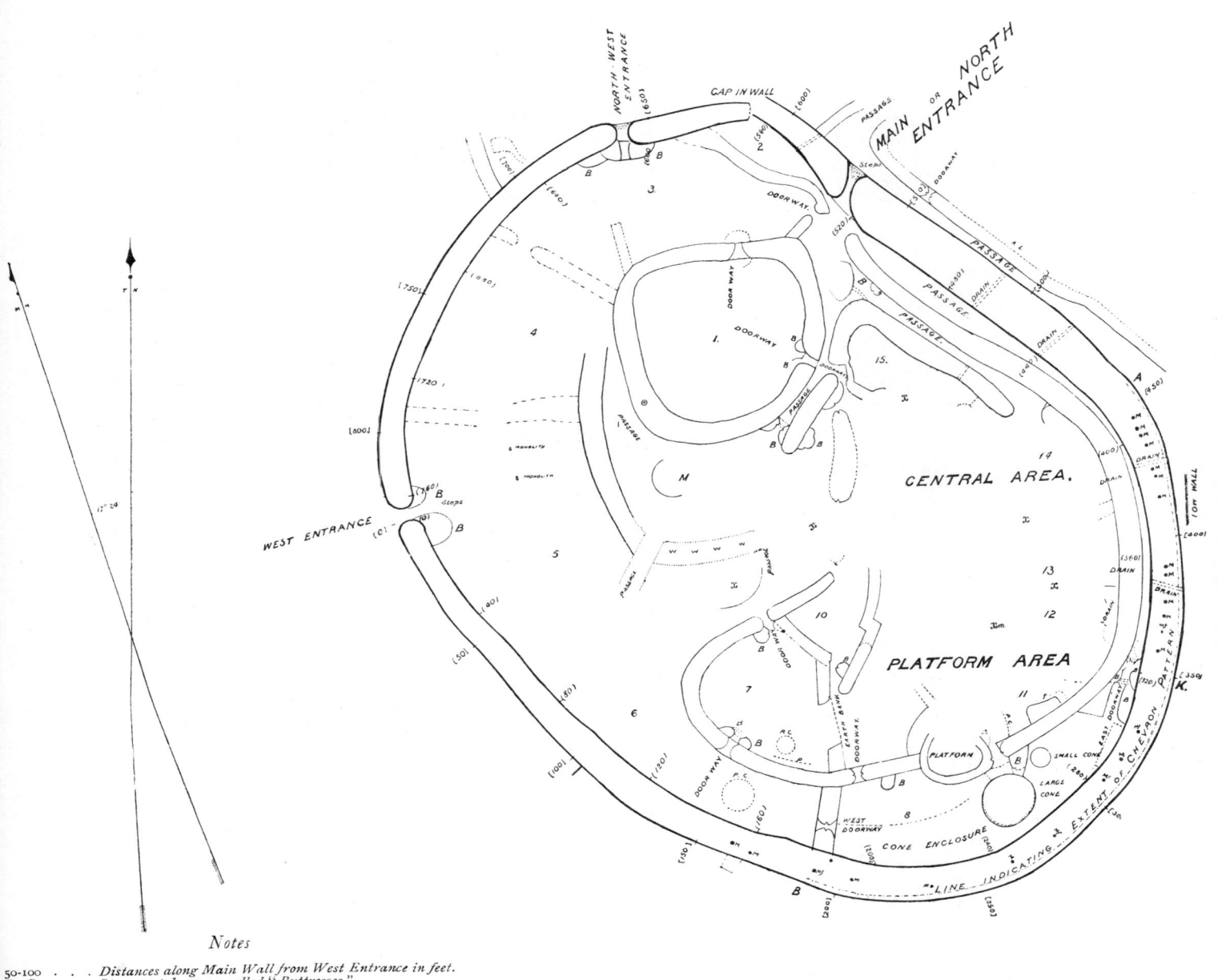

Notes

50-100	Distances along Main Wall from West Entrance in feet.
B. B.	Stone protuberances called "Buttresses."
M Mf	Small stone "monoliths" on top of Main Wall. f, fallen.
1, 3	Numbers given to Enclosures.
DRAINS	Small holes through walls.
Steps	Shown in lines of small dots.
Broken lines	Old foundations or ruined walls.
W. W. W. W.	Conjectural Restoration of line of wall.
———	Decorated portion of Outer Wall.
A. B. K. M.	Points referred to in Bent's "Ruined Cities."
P. C.	Circles or benches covered with plaster or cement.
x, x	Conjectural positions of cement platforms.
xm	The cement platform decorated with monoliths.

SCALE 50 FEET TO 1 INCH.

THE GREAT ZIMBABWE, PLAN OF THE ELLIPTICAL RUIN.

See pages 67-74.

PLATE XXVI.

(a) FAÇADE OF THE "ELLIPTICAL TEMPLE," ZIMBABWE. *See page* 69.

(b) INTERIOR OF THE "ELLIPTICAL TEMPLE," ZIMBABWE. THE CONICAL TOWER. *See page* 73.

PLATE XXVII.

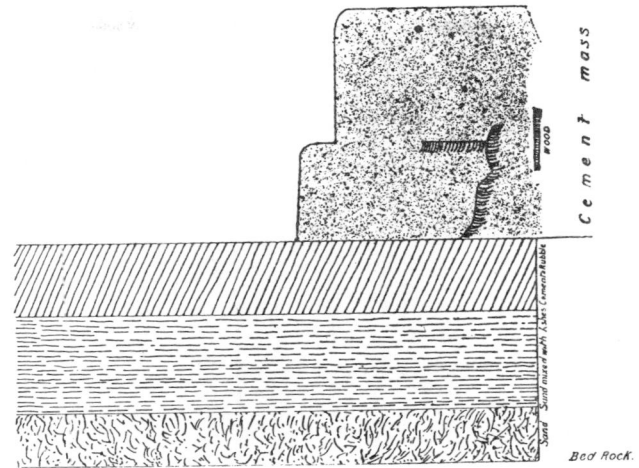

(a) SECTION OF ENCLOSURE XV. IN THE "ELLIPTICAL TEMPLE," ZIMBABWE. (SCALE 1 : 60.)

See pages 61-63.

(b) PHOTOGRAPH OF THE SAME SECTION FROM THE RUBBLE AND CEMENT FLOOR UPWARDS.

See pages 61-63.

CHAPTER IX

ZIMBABWE.   THE VALLEY RUINS.   THE ACROPOLIS.   OBJECTS FOUND

The "Valley Ruins" (Plate XXVIII) extend for about three-quarters of a mile in a line from east to west and occupy the southern side of the valley that separates the "Elliptical Temple" from the "Acropolis." The most extensive portion of them is that series of buildings adjoining the northern side of the "Temple" commonly called "No. 1 Ruins." To the north-east of these are the "Renders" and the "Posselt Ruins," immediately east of which again are the "Philips" and the "Maund Ruins," and, standing a little apart like an outpost station, the "East Ruins."

<small>The Valley Ruins.</small>

The relation of these buildings to the others is not difficult to surmise. The "Temple" being the royal residence, these are no doubt the dwellings of the chief persons in the tribe. They are unfortified, since the impregnable "Acropolis" was close at hand for any occasion when a city of refuge was needed. In the valley, then, no doubt, lived those wealthy traders who received the gold brought in from neighbouring districts and bartered it with Arab merchants from the east coast.[18] Actual mining operations were not carried on at Zimbabwe, for there is little or no trace there of anything connected with the preliminary processes of crushing, washing, and retorting. All this must have been done at the more distant places where the gold was found, and whence it was brought by caravans to the capital.[19] Zimbabwe itself was simply the distributing centre. No unmelted gold is found in the ruins, though small trinkets, wire, tacks foil, and beads have been turned out in considerable quantities at one time and another. Possibly the gold beads were a sort of currency, for we read in a Portuguese report of the year 1513 that "all the gold brought to Sofala is wrought into very small beads," and that when any king sent a gift to the captain of Sofala it would be "a bunch of very small beads of gold." (*T.R.* i. 81, 82.)

76 MEDIÆVAL RHODESIA

Zimbabwe.

The Valley Ruins.

The buildings are quite of a kind to suggest that their occupants were men of wealth and position. No trouble or expense was spared in their construction. The granite bed-rock was covered with a cement pavement, as much as two metres thick in some places, to make a level and dry foundation; and upon this were erected walls of which the masonry is often as good as that in the "Temple."

Philips Ruins.

A view of part of the "Philips Ruins" (Plate XXVIII. b) will perhaps give the best idea of the Zimbabwe style in general. In the immediate foreground of the picture is the characteristic rounded entrance, a groove in the side of which doubtless once contained an upright stone beam, like one which still stands in its original place in a doorway a few yards away. Such wedge-shaped slits, indeed, are to be seen everywhere in the sides of the doorways, and have sometimes, by an absurd misinterpretation, been termed "portcullis grooves." Numerous plain stone beams have been found in various parts of the "Valley Ruins," and some of them at least must have stood originally in the doorways, though only one is now to be seen *in situ*. The height of this beam—double that of the wall—and its shape show that the doorway cannot have been lintelled with a stone slab as was done on the Acropolis.

It was in the Philips Ruins, near the main or eastern wall, but at a point which he does not precisely indicate, that Mr. R. N. Hall found a soapstone beam finely carved with the figures of a bird and of a crocodile, and with the chevron pattern. Through the entrance there appears a low cylinder of masonry, the purpose of which I am wholly unable to explain; and on the right of this, but not appearing in the photograph, are still standing parts of the cement walls of one of the original huts. Behind the cylinder the elliptical buttress of a doorway joining an angle of wall exemplifies a peculiarity of the Rhodesian buildings, viz. that walls are hardly ever bonded in to one another. The cement covering or dado on the stone in the same place is a curious feature, which recurs occasionally at Khami. On the left of the picture are typical low tiers or steps of cement, bevelled on the face, which lead up to a cement hut-foundation. In the background of the picture, to the right, appears a part of the Maund Ruins.

The Acropolis.

Of the third part of the Zimbabwe Ruins, namely, the "Acropolis," it is almost impossible to give a detailed description. A hill that rises precipitously to a height of from 200 feet to 300 feet above the valley, which it bounds for a distance of about three-quarters of a mile, has been converted by the ingenuity of the builders into an absolutely impregnable stronghold. Much of the work had already been done by nature, and the engineers of the negro capital neglected no opportunity which nature offered them. Where granite boulders had already outlined an enclosure, they adapted their plan to the form thus suggested to them and completed the apartment with masonry. Clefts have been converted into passages, jutting crags enlarged into platforms, and gigantic rocks utilised to form the bases of artificial walls. It is a labyrinth approached by two tortuous paths, which begin some distance inside the low wall encircling the hill, and wind up the south-east and north-west sides to the summit.

<small>The Acropolis</small>

The Acropolis has never been exhaustively explored, and the next excavator who may happen to work at Zimbabwe will probably find this a less unremunerative field than the "Elliptical Temple" or "Valley Ruins." On the hillside are very large beds of debris thrown out by the old inhabitants, which would certainly yield a considerable quantity of objects, though of course their very extent decreases the immediate probability of coming on many valuable or interesting things in a short time.

Much, too, remains to be done here, as well as in other parts of the site, by a really patient and conscientious researcher if he is willing to devote a good many months to the study and comparison of minute details, with a view to explaining the purpose of the various enclosures and apartments.

As the limited time at my disposal forbade my undertaking excavations upon the Acropolis, I shall content myself with making a few remarks upon one, perhaps, however, the most interesting, of the enclosures which it contains. It is that which is commonly referred to as the "Western Temple," an irregular, more or less horseshoe-shaped, apartment. Plate XXIX. *a* shows the exterior southern wall, a fine piece of dry masonry, which is continued along the summit of the sheer precipice. The exterior wall of this "Temple" was decorated all round, in the same style as the façade of the "Elliptical Temple" in the valley, with monoliths of granite and slate, of which a few still remain. Four that stand on the top of the southern section of the wall form a conspicuous feature in the view of the Acropolis from the valley. Their appearance may be understood from the photograph in Plate XXIX.*b*, which shows two others on the eastern side. The western section of the wall was further ornamented with a series of small round towers alternating with the monoliths. The best preserved of these is 1.07 m. in height, with a diameter at the top of 1.0 m.; it is built with a slight batter.

<small>Western Temple on the Acropolis.</small>

The resemblance of this enclosure to the "Elliptical Temple" does not,

Zimbabwe.

Western Temple on the Acropolis.

however, end with its exterior decoration. The arrangement of the interior strongly recalls that of the ceremonial portion of the "Elliptical Temple." Here, as there, is a cement dais facing outward to the entrance (Plate XXIX.*b*, centre), and with a separate approach to it. In front of the dais, and precisely in the same relative position as the platform decorated with monoliths in the "Elliptical Temple," is a shallow, circular platform, which may well have served the same purpose as an altar or an accessory of some solemn observance.

It was from this enclosure that Mr. Bent removed the four famous soapstone beams carved at the top with figures of birds. It seems that they, probably with two or three others, stood here, though at what particular point is uncertain. I had already suggested that the bird, which resembles an eagle or vulture, might represent the tribal emblem, and have quite recently learned that a tribe in the Belingwe district actually has an eagle as its sacred animal.

It may be conjectured, therefore, that the "Western Temple" on the Acropolis, like the "Elliptical Temple" in the Valley, was a place of solemn assembly, into which the chief entered on solemn occasions and seated himself on the dais of state. Beside him would have been his great men, and round him the most sacred symbols of the tribe.

Objects found at Zimbabwe.

The objects which we discovered in the course of excavations at the Great Zimbabwe, though not of the same intrinsic value as some which, it is rumoured, have rewarded the search of certain gold-seekers in past days, are of great archæological interest. With one or two small exceptions (pp. 63, 87, 88), everything was found in the "Valley Ruins." First in order comes the metal-work, to obtain a satisfactory account of which I submitted a number of sample specimens to the expert analysis of Mr. G. A. Pingstone. His report is as follows :—

Report by Mr. G. A. Pingstone, F.C.S.
Analyst to the Bulawayo Municipal Council, etc.

"I have carefully examined the parcel of bangles, wire, and metallic remains recovered from Zimbabwe.

"I have classified and labelled certain typical specimens, according to composition, as follows :—

"No. 1. *Gold.*—In the form of thin, spirally-coiled wire. Weight, 106 grains.

"No. 2. *Copper.*—As wire, portions of bangles. The very fine wire is in nearly every case Copper.

"No. 3. *Bronze*.—As wire and ribbon coiled round a core of vegetable fibre to form bangles. A piece of 'foil with tacks' is also Bronze.

"No. 3A. *Bronze ribbon* made into bangles or portions of bangles, as No. 3, but having a distinct coating on the outside of green or bluish-green glaze.

"This glaze is vitreous and silicious. The colour is due to Copper and a little Iron in a sample I tested.

"From all appearances this glaze would appear to have been applied after the bangle had been manufactured, as it appears to be only on the outside of the coiled ribbon and to fill up the interstices between the wrapping. Had the ribbon been coated before wrapping, one would have expected it to crack off when coiled. Against this theory there is, however, the fact that the fibre core would have been destroyed had the articles been subjected to any considerable heat in the process of glazing. I am convinced that this is a glass and not a paint, as it is quite transparent. It should not be difficult, therefore, to ascertain the origin of this class of ware if it is a more or less ancient trade commodity, as one must come to the conclusion that it is.[19]

"Beyond the Bronze Glazed bangles there is nothing of any great interest in the other articles, but I might mention that the split Bronze bangle composed of one coarse wire is distinctly magnetic, and probably has a certain amount of Iron in its composition."

Specimens of each of the classes of metal-work described by Mr. Pingstone are figured in Plate XXX. In the left-hand bottom corner (No. 28) is a little cap of gold which had been nailed on to wood, possibly as the covering of a wand. Beside it (No. 27) is the oblong packet of spirally-coiled wire mentioned in the report. Beside these is a bangle of twisted copper (No. 29) and a coil of copper wire (No. 30). No. 24 is the piece of bronze foil with tacks, and Nos. 25 and 26 are two bronze bangles, one of coiled wire and the other solid. Nos. 21, 22, and 23 are three specimens of the enamelled bronze ribbon, No. 21 being a damaged piece, selected in order to show the vegetable fibre clearly. A fragment of similar ribbon has been examined in England by Prof. W. Gowland, who reports: "The green coating of the copper spiral contains copper carbonate and silicious matter. It is not the result of weathering, but has been artificially applied by means of some organic medium and not by fusion."

80   MEDIÆVAL RHODESIA

Zimbabwe.

Objects found there.

4. *Iron.*—Besides this finer metal-work, most of which came from "Renders Ruins," we found iron bangles and numerous implements and weapons of iron. The latter in general resemble the types found at Inyanga and Umtali; the most characteristic are figured in Plate XXXI.

5. *Faience*—very valuable for dating purposes. The most beautiful is a piece of Oriental Faience figured in the lower left-hand corner of XXX. *a* (8). It came from "Renders Ruins," and belonged to the same vase of which Mr. R. N. Hall had previously found six fragments. I have included the latter in my photograph, in order to exhibit the patterns and the lettering.

The inscription is in Persian; the larger letters are too much broken to be decipherable, but the smaller writing which appears on the fragment in Plate XXX. 7 can be read as "Tarikh mah Shawwal," *i.e.* "date month Shawwal." The month Shawwal is the tenth in the Mohammedan year; it is most unfortunate that the piece is broken exactly where the year itself would have been entered. However, the vessel can be approximately dated even without that exact statement. Among four Persian scholars who independently examined the writing as shown in my photograph, there was a consensus of opinion that it could not be earlier at any rate than the fifteenth century, A.D., and three of them went so far as to say it could not be earlier than the sixteenth.

On the other hand, Mr. C. H. Read, as will be seen from his note at the close of this chapter, judging the fabric as an archæologist, would assign it to the fourteenth or just possibly to the thirteenth century. In that case this Persian faience and the Arabic glass found by Mr. R. N. Hall would be the earliest of all the objects ever obtained from Zimbabwe.

In the East Ruins we found a piece of thick stoneware glazed with white and green, resembling a fragment found at Umtali (pp. 86, 104).

6. *Glass.*—Some fragments of thin, green glass were found in "Renders Ruins" and in "No. 1 Ruins."

7. *Beads.*—A number of small, brilliantly-coloured glass beads were found in "Renders Ruins." They were lying loose in the soil, and the illustration in Plate XXX. *a*, No. 2, shows a somewhat speculative restoration. The native women at the present day string up the Italian beads sold them by European traders in exactly the same fashion as they used to in mediæval days, according to the accounts preserved to us.

THE VALLEY RUINS. THE ACROPOLIS. OBJECTS FOUND

Objects found at Zimbabwe.

Moreover, the patterns are the same as in those times. Accordingly, I handed some of the loose beads from "Renders Ruins" to a Makalanga woman, and told her to make them up into such a necklace as she had just sold me for a shilling. The result was the piece of pattern-work shown in Plate XXX. *a*, No. 2.

Some large glass beads were found in several places ("Renders Ruins," "East Ruins"); they are described below by Mr. C. H. Read.

8. One or two small *soapstone objects*, including two phalli ("No. 1 Ruins").
9. *Earthenware pottery* of two kinds—viz. rough unornamented household pottery, hand-made, and varnished with plumbago. Wheel-made pottery unvarnished, but ornamented with incised geometrical patterns; inferior in style to the pottery from any of the other sites.

Also pottery spindle-whorls and small pottery figures of cattle.*

It will be observed that there is nothing antique amongst these objects, so that the Valley Ruins, like the Elliptical Temple, are mediæval.

Some of the most typical dating objects from the various ruins were submitted for examination to Mr. C. H. Read, Keeper of the Ethnological Department of the British Museum, who has very kindly furnished the following report upon them :—

"1. A fragment of a Persian faience vessel with metallic lustre outside, painted in blue and green within. This, in common with the other fragments of the same ware, probably dates from the fourteenth century, though it may be a century earlier. It agrees in date with the fragments of Arab glass I have seen from the ruins. (Plate XXX. 8.) Zimbabwe.

"2. *a*. Two fragments of Chinese porcelain painted in blue under glaze; the style of decoration and tint of blue indicate the middle of the Ming dynasty, about early sixteenth century. (Plate XXX. 11.) Dhlo-Dhlo.

"β. A small piece of silver with punched ornament—probably Arab.

'3. *a*. Fragment of a small bowl or cup of Chinese porcelain, covered with Khami.

---

* All the objects found at Zimbabwe are in the Bulawayo Museum, and are marked with letters and numbers showing their exact provenance. These identification marks are as follows :—

Z.E. = "Zimbabwe Elliptical Temple," any number following being that of the enclosure, thus—

Z.E. 15 = "Zimbabwe Elliptical Temple, Enclosure 15" (the word "Ash" following this means the stratum of sand mixed with ashes in the section described on pp. 61-64).

Z.R. = "Zimbabwe, Renders Ruins."

Z. Ridge = "Zimbabwe, No. 1 Ruins."

Z. = "Zimbabwe, East Ruins."

a delicate pale-blue celadon glaze; it is ornamented with vertical furrows inside and out. Probably sixteenth century; the Persians copied this style of bowl in the following century.

Dhlo-Dhlo. "β. Two specimens of glass, amber-coloured and clear. Probably Arab, but impossible to determine more nearly.

Zimbabwe. "4. Seven beads of green glass of the size of a pea and a number of minute ones. The larger are made on a mandril, and might well have been made in Egypt or elsewhere in the Mediterranean area. Date uncertain.

Dhlo-Dhlo. "5. Fifteen glass beads of various sorts. Of these one is almost certainly of fairly modern Venetian make. It is made from a 'cane' of clear green glass with an opaque-red outer lining. Similar beads occur among the treasure of beads secured from Prempeh's house at Kumasi; among the spoils of a wreck on the Irish coast about 1820, and among a number of miscellaneous beads from the East brought by Rev. Greville J. Chester. All these latter are in the British Museum.

"The edge of a dish shown on Plate XXX. No. 20 would appear to be of the seventeenth century, without doubt; but I have not seen the original."

PLATE XXVIII.

(a) GENERAL VIEW OF THE VALLEY RUINS, ZIMBABWE.   *See pages* 75, 76.

(b) VIEW OF THE PHILIPS RUINS IN THE VALLEY, ZIMBABWE.   *See pages* 75, 76.

PLATE XXIX.

GENERAL VIEW OF THE ACROPOLIS, ZIMBABWE.   *See page 77.*

PART OF THE WESTERN TEMPLE, ACROPOLIS, ZIMBABWE.   *See pages 77, 78.*

PLATE XXX.

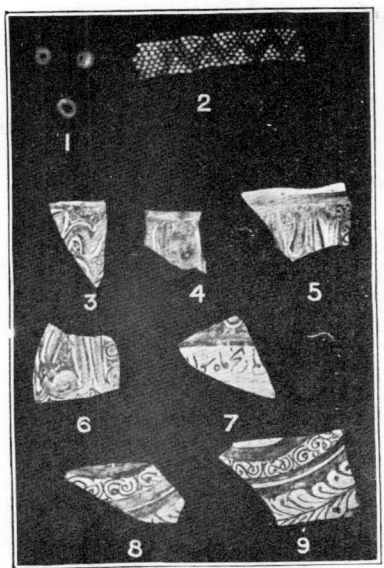

ORIENTAL FAIENCE FROM ZIMBABWE.
See page 80.

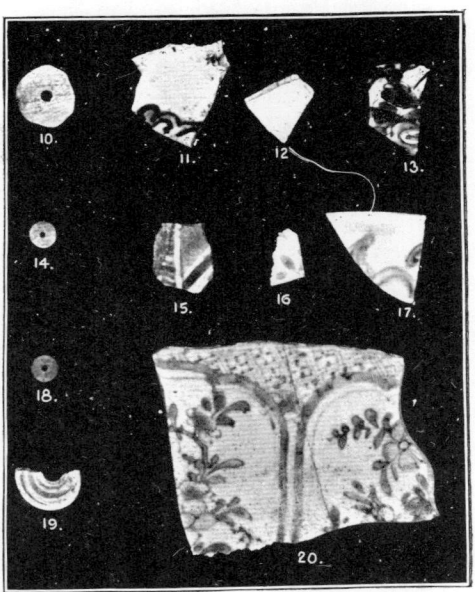

CHINA AND IVORY AND SHELL BEADS FOUND AT DHLO-DHLO.
See pages 43, 45, 46.

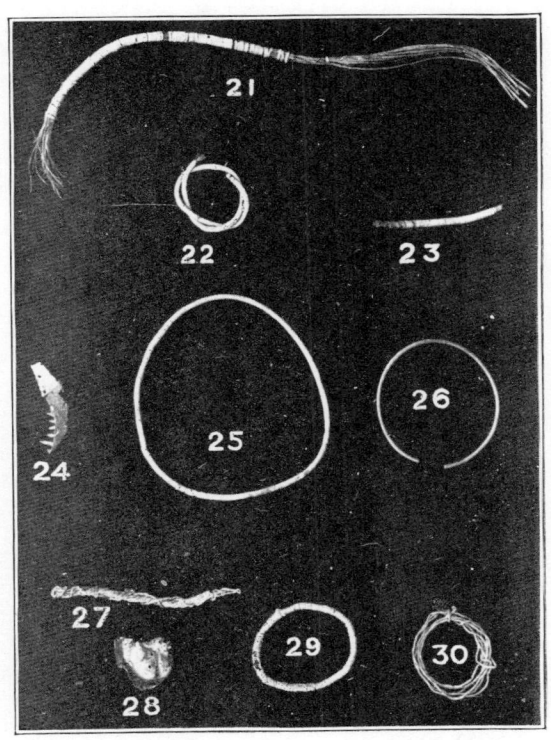

GOLD, COPPER, BRONZE, AND ENAMELLED BRONZE FROM ZIMBABWE.
See page 79.

PLATE XXXI.

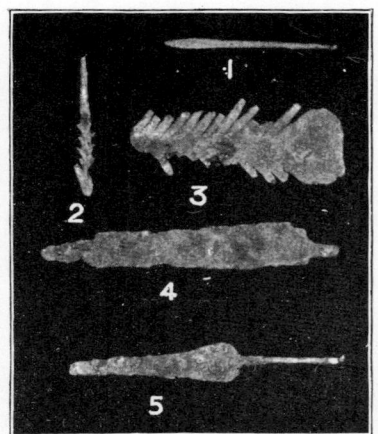
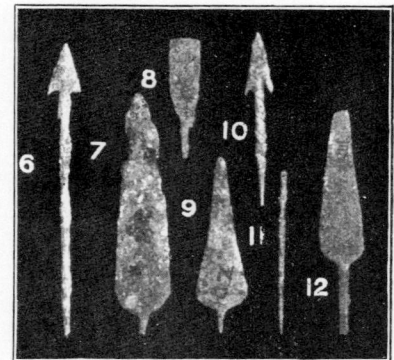
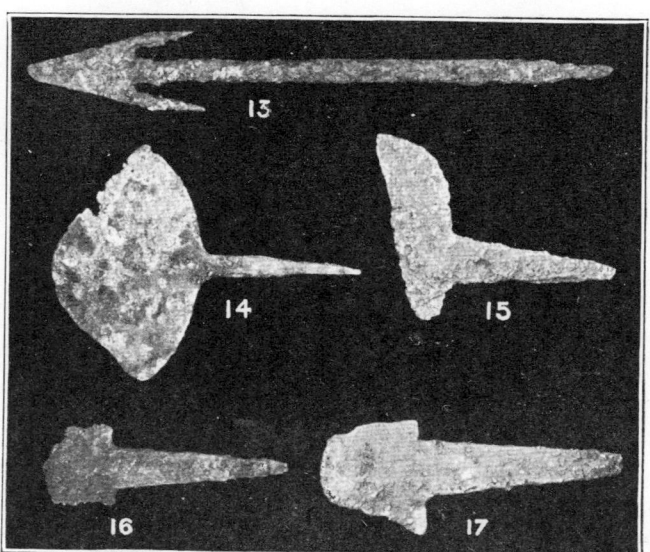
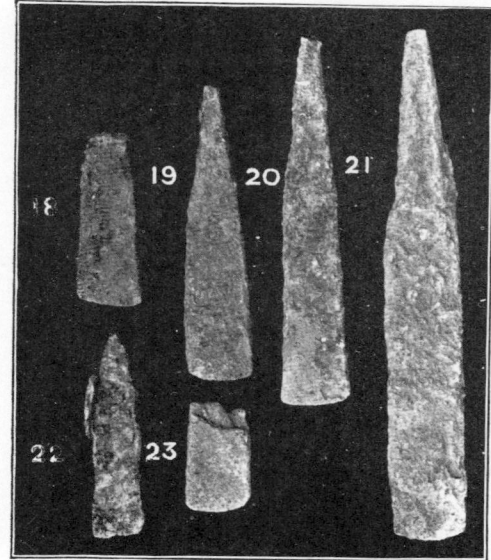
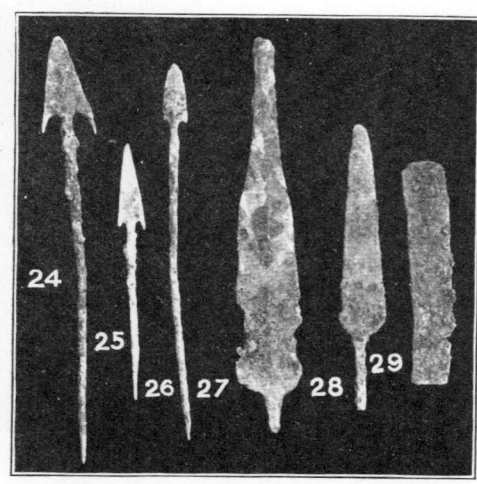

IRON WEAPONS, ZIMBABWE.

See page 79.

PLATE XXXII.

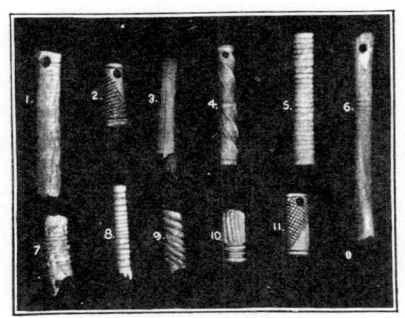

BONE AMULETS FROM KHAMI.

See page 58.

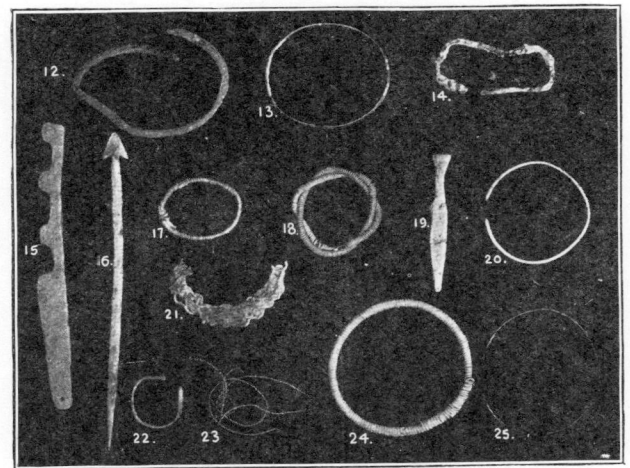

IRON, COPPER, AND BRONZE ARTICLES FROM KHAMI.

See page 58.

CHAPTER X

CONCLUSION

THE account of exploration and excavation being finished, it remains briefly to recapitulate the main results arrived at, and to gather them into a coherent whole.

Seven sites have been investigated, and from not one of them has any object been obtained by myself or by others before me which can be shown to be more ancient than the fourteenth or fifteenth century A.D.

In the architecture, whether military or domestic, there is not a trace of Oriental or European style of any period whatever.

Not a single inscription has ever been found in the country.

So much for the negative side. On the positive side I hope that I have succeeded in showing

(1) That imported articles, of which the date is well known in the country of their origin, are contemporary with the Rhodesian buildings in which they are found, and that these buildings are therefore mediæval and post-mediæval.

(2) That the character of the dwellings contained within the stone ruins, and forming an integral part of them, is unmistakably African.

(3) That the arts and manufactures exemplified by objects found within these dwellings are typically African, except when the objects are imports of well-known mediæval or post-mediæval date.

The main proof of the first of these points is to be found in the chapters dealing with excavations at Dhlo-Dhlo and at Zimbabwe (Chaps. V., VII., IX.).

That of the second and third points is to be found in every chapter where I describe the dwellings of the ruin-builders from Inyanga to Zimbabwe. But a few lines may be added to guard against any possible misconceptions.

There is no difference whatever in essential character between the rough buildings that are found in the Inyanga district and those of the Monomotapan capital near Victoria. Zimbabwe reproduces every feature of the northern sites, only with more elaboration and on a huger scale. The "Elliptical Temple" can be completely explained as a combination of the developed form of Inyanga hill-fort with such a stone-fenced kraal as Nanatali.

How closely the dwellings themselves and the articles found in them resemble those of the modern natives is sufficiently shown by the mere fact that an untrained and inexperienced excavator has mistaken the one for the other. Those, moreover, who have only had the opportunity of seeing one or two "ancient" buildings have always observed the resemblance, but have been content with the wholly unsupported assertion that "Kaffirs" had recently squatted there. But I hope to have demonstrated by my field work—firstly, that the supposed productions of the modern natives are found in positions where they cannot be later than the first stones of the building itself; secondly, that the huts occur in so many widely separated localities, and with such invariable persistency over every part of a site, and form so inseparable a part of the structure in each case, that no theory of reoccupation can explain them. On the Niekerk Ruins the hut-foundations are found in every quarter of an area so vast that the entire population of the surrounding district far and wide would not now suffice to occupy it. The stone rings fit into every corner of the platform or enclosure upon or within which they stand; and when made of rubble and clay the hut-foundations are often so built as to be actually continuous parts of the stone walls.

In the citadel of Dhlo-Dhlo the cement platforms make a perfectly indivisible mass; they rest against the encircling stone wall at every point, and the sides of the huts erected upon them form an unbroken vertical line with the top tier of the façade. At Nanatali the "witch-doctor's hut" is an inseparable part of the elliptical girdle-wall, and the chief's hut in the centre is connected by stone walls with the decorated front. At Zimbabwe the immense beds of cement which are built up in the interior into platforms run underneath the stone walls themselves. In short, there is nothing inside the walls anywhere which is not either the foundation of a hut or the foundation of a building constructed like a hut. It is, properly speaking, the huts which constitute the really essential part of the ruin in every case; the stone wall which the visitor so much admires is only the skin, the huts are the flesh and bone.

CONCLUSION

These dwellings, then, found everywhere within the stone enclosures, and inseparable from them, are unquestionably African in every detail, and belong to a period which is fixed by foreign imports as in general mediæval. There is one last refuge for those who cannot deny the African origin of the Rhodesian ruins and yet refuse to believe that negroes can have built them. The negroes built them, these theorists suggest, but under the dominance of a foreign race. To this the answer is easy. The *onus probandi* lies with those who advance a view for which there is not a particle of evidence. Where are the traces of this foreign race? And again, this theory actually conflicts with documentary evidence. For if my dating of the ruins is accepted, the Portuguese chronicles become available as contemporary, or almost contemporary, records. But the Portuguese writers give no hint of any domination of the negroes by an alien race. On the contrary, De Barros and De Goes explicitly state that the inhabitants of the district round the Monomotapan capital were woolly-haired negroes. And the missionary who records the conversion to Christianity of a Monomotapa at his Zimbabwe near Masapa in the middle of the seventeenth century, states explicitly that he was a black man ("*con carnes pretas*"). So that there is not only no reason for accepting this gratuitous theory, but there is good reason for refusing to entertain it at all.[20]

As to which particular tribe of negroes erected the buildings I make no suggestion. It is for those who live in the country and have an intimate knowledge of the natives to attack that problem. And indications are not wanting to show that if sufficient interest is taken in it the problem will shortly be solved.

Having established their native origin and general period, I may now attempt to fix more closely the relative antiquity of the several sites and make some suggestions regarding their history.

The importance of Zimbabwe seems to centre around the beginning of the sixteenth century A.D. The earliest *possible date* for any of its buildings is two centuries before this. That is to say, they belong to the time when Sofala was a flourishing port, inhabited by a colony of Arabs who traded with the interior for gold. They brought in exchange the products of the East, and perhaps some of the manufactures of Europe, which came by way of Cairo, where, since the days of the Crusades, Italian merchants had been established.

But I have shown that it is possible that a slightly earlier settlement may have existed at Zimbabwe, although none of the buildings now standing can be attributed to it. It would be absurd to suggest that this hypothetical settlement antedated the buildings by any great length of time, but it may be allowed perhaps to extend the antiquity of the site, simply as an inhabited site, by a century or two. And as Zimbabwe, being the great distributing centre, must have owed its very existence to that trade with the coast first opened up by the Arabs of Magadoxo, the *earliest possible* date for *any* settlement there is the eleventh century A.D.

As the prosperity and wealth of the community increased, the two great strongholds, the Acropolis and the Elliptical Temple, were built, and the rich traders erected their luxurious houses in the valley between.

With the last years of the fifteenth century, the Portuguese came to the east coast and established a trading station, and soon afterwards a fort at Sofala (1506), though transacting most of their business with the interior indirectly through the medium of Arab merchants. For two or three generations Sofala flourished more than ever before, then gradually declined owing to the preponderance of Mozambique and the growing importance of the Portuguese settlements on the Zambesi. At just the same time the paramountcy of the negro chief called the Monomotapa was impaired by the rebellion of various vassal lords; he lost much of the southern part of his dominion, and retired to a contracted realm and another capital on the Mazoe.

And from that time the Great Zimbabwe must have lost its importance; in the seventeenth century it may still have existed, but no longer as an important place. Some one of those terrible waves of devastating conquerors which have swept over South Africa periodically as long as we have any knowledge of its history, may have blotted the inhabitants off the face of the earth and left the city to fall into ruins.[21]

But in other districts new capitals, less magnificent but not less interesting, sprang into existence. Dhlo-Dhlo and Nanatali were probably not even founded until Zimbabwe had ceased to be the residence of the Monomotapa, and Khami I should judge to be contemporary with these fortress-kraals of the Insiza district.

The oldest remains in the country appear to be those of the northern district between Inyanga and the Zambesi. The difficulty of precisely dating these has been already mentioned, but now that the antiquity of the better known sites has been ascertained, the Inyanga and Niekerk Ruins can be assigned to their proper place.

Umtali constitutes a valuable link between Zimbabwe and Inyanga. Various small indications inclined me to suppose from the first that the rough stone buildings at Umtali were about four or five hundred years old. A fragment of glazed stoneware discovered near the Umtali altar, and closely resembling stoneware found at Zimbabwe, confirms this view. When we consider further that there is, at any rate as yet, no evidence of actual Portuguese trade with Umtali, that site may fairly be considered to belong to the fifteenth century.[22]

Inyanga and the Niekerk Ruins, to judge from the evolution of the form of buildings, should be slightly earlier than Umtali. The primitive character of the pottery is not in itself conclusive, but certainly does to some extent corroborate this suggestion. The negative evidence, however, showing the total absence of Portuguese trade with a district which was in the immediate neighbourhood of the sixteenth century Portuguese forts near the Zambesi, is very valuable. It suggests that the Inyanga and Nani settlements were deserted by about 1550 A.D., if not earlier.

Considering that the immense system of intrenchment which I have described as existing in those parts must have taken even a large population some time to complete, it would be reasonable to ascribe the forts and dwellings of Inyanga and the Niekerk Ruins to the two or three centuries preceding 1500 A.D.

That is to say, they would be older than the actual ruins of the Great Zimbabwe near Victoria, and contemporary with the slightly earlier settlement which I have suggested may have existed there before the ruins. Probably the Inyanga and Nani districts were deserted in consequence of some such devastating inroad as that of the historical Zimbas.

Some who may have been convinced by my reasoning will yet have been convinced against their will, and many no doubt will bewail that a romance has been destroyed. But surely it is a prosaic mind that sees no romance in the partial opening of this new chapter in the history of vanished cultures. A corner is lifted of that veil which has shrouded the forgotten but not irrecoverable past of the African negro. Were I a Rhodesian I should feel that in studying the contemporary natives in order to unravel the story of the ruins I had a task as romantic as any student could desire. I should feel that in studying the ruins in order thereby to gain a knowledge of the modern races I had an interest that the politician should support and that the scholar must envy.

APPENDIX I

DETAILS OF TRIAL-SECTIONS IN THE ELLIPTICAL TEMPLE, ZIMBABWE

In Chapter VII. the most important section which we cut in the Elliptical Temple has been minutely described. It may be well to give brief notes upon the other trial-sections and soundings which we sunk within the same building.

Section 2.—In the "south passage," at a distance of 6.60 m. from the centre of the bay of "Enclosure 15," on its exterior (*i.e.* northern) side, we sunk a pit 1.40 m. deep exactly opposite to the north-east entrance. The top of the pit began at the cement floor forming the foundation of the northern wall of "Enclosure 1." After passing through 0.30 m. of cement and rubble we struck grey sand, in which no objects were found below the topmost ten centimetres (potsherds). At 1.40 m. came on bed-rock.

From this section it may be inferred that the layer of ashes mixed with sand, which was formed within Enclosure 15, does not extend beyond there, at any rate on this side.

Section 3.—Within "Enclosure 3" a pit was sunk at 7.0 m. south-east of the "north-west entrance." The top of it was virtually on a level with the first step of the entrance. It showed at the top a thickness of 0.40 m. of cement, below which was 0.90 m. of sand, then bed-rock.

Immediately below the cement were found a portion of a spindle-whorl, fragments of the ordinary plain household pottery, and a fragment of such coiled iron wire as was found in the "Renders Ruins."

Section 4.—In "Enclosure 1," at the north end (in the northern corner), close against the wall, the top was 0.70 m. below the top course of the steps of the passage on the north side. The pit passed through 0.20 of cement, then 1.10 m. of sand, striking bed-rock at 1.30 m.

The only objects found were a few fragments of plain household pottery just below the cement.

APPENDIX I

Section 5.—In "Enclosure 5" we dug a trench from the "west entrance," which passed between the two standing monoliths to the cover where the boundary wall of "Enclosure 5" meets the wall of the "west passage."

The top of the trench was 0.50 m. below the level of the floor of the "west entrance." Passed through 0.40 m. of cement, then 0.20 m. of rubble, after which got into natural sand, and discontinued at 0.30 m. lower. Depth of our trench, 0.90 m.; did not reach bed-rock.

At the level of the rubble found fragments of the usual plain household pottery, one iron spearhead, two fragments of white porcelain. No objects below the rubble, the sand being evidently the original native soil.

Section 6.—Dug a section in "Enclosure 6" at 6.50 m. north of the northern wall of Enclosure 7.

The top started at the same level as the section in Enclosure 5. Passed through 0.60 m. of cement, then through grey sand to a farther depth of 0.70 m. Found a long iron spear-head just below the surface, but no other objects. Deepening the trench at its eastern end we found that the sand was evidently undisturbed, and that it went down over a metre more without touching bed-rock.

Section 7.—In "Enclosure 12" dug a trench across the platform, which is immediately on the left of the famous "Platform" (or "Dais," as I have sometimes called it) as we look southwards facing the "Cone." The top started 0.40 m. below the top of the cement dado on the wall. Passed through cement, which was 1.0 m. in thickness, at a distance of 5.50 m. from the wall of the "parallel passage," but decreased to 0.70 m. north of this point, forming a step in the platform. Sinking to a total depth of 2.30 m. at 5.50 m. distance north of the wall of the "parallel passage," we were still in the grey sand, which is immediately under the cement, and had not reached bed-rock. The sand had evidently never been disturbed.

No objects of any kind were found in this section.

APPENDIX II

Note 1.—**Guillain's** work is entitled *Documents sur l'histoire, la géographie, et le commerce de l'Afrique Orientale* (Paris, Bertrand, 1856), and ranks as a standard authority. It is in three volumes, of which the second and third record the results of the author's own explorations. The first volume contains an admirable treatise on the whole subject of the geography and history of East Africa from the earliest times down to the middle of the nineteenth century. The detailed critiques of the early geographers are especially valuable.

Strandes' *Die Portugusiesenzeit von Deutsch- und Englisch-Ost Afrika* (Berlin, Reimer, 1899) is a book of less compass, but gives a clear and well-written account of the period with which it deals.

Theal's *Records of South-Eastern Africa* is of the very highest value, and should be in the hands of every one who is interested in the subject. It is a collection of all the original documents (mainly Portuguese) relating to South-Eastern Africa, accompanied by a trustworthy English translation. Published in nine volumes at the expense of the Government of Cape Colony, it contains not only State correspondence, letters of missionaries, accounts of shipwrecks, etc., but also the writings of historians, such as Duarte Barbosa, De Goes, De Barros, and Dos Santos, which are not easy of access in any other form. Only one thing is needed to make it complete, and that is a study of the topography. The publication of a series of the mediæval maps accompanied by a commentary would be a great boon to students.

There has been occasion to cite Dr. Theal's work very frequently; and for brevity's sake I have referred to it always by the letters *T.R.*, followed by the number and page of the volume. In most cases it has been considered sufficient to give the reference only to the English translation, leaving the reader to turn up the Portuguese original, which always precedes it by a few pages. But when the passage is one of first-rate importance I have given a double reference, the first to the English version, the second to the Portuguese. The following sentence may serve as an example:—"*The Chronicle of Kilwa*

APPENDIX II—NOTES

is preserved in the historian João de Barros, and may be found in *T.R.* vi. pp. 233, 240-244, and pp. 80, 87-90."

Note 2.—**Loopholes.**—It may be well to remark that Kaffir tribes with whom the Portuguese had encounters used loopholes in their earthworks (see *T.R.* iii. 363, 390; vii. 294).

Note 3.—**Portuguese Forts.**—It is not likely to be seriously suggested that these hill-forts of the Inyanga district were built by the Portuguese, but it may not be amiss to point out—first, that all Portuguese stone forts were rectangular; secondly, that they built no forts of *stone*, but only of palisaded wood, south of the Zambesi, except at Sofala; thirdly, that they never penetrated to the Inyanga region. The chief references for the topography of the Portuguese "fairs" and forts are as follows: *T.R.* i. 23, 81, 396; ii. 412, 414, 417; iii. 354; iv. 72, 305, 343, 423; vi. 368, 369; vii. 270.

Note 4.—**Walls in the Inyanga District.**— A Bulawayo correspondent, Mr. J. M. Mowbray, communicates a native story with regard to certain of the walls in the Inyanga district. It is to the effect that the natives at one time were greatly troubled by rhinoceroses which raided their grain-gardens and destroyed their crops. The natives therefore took to the hills, and, by making series of terraces, were enabled to keep off the rhinoceroses and to cultivate the hillsides. When the Portuguese came into the country and supplied them with guns the Kaffirs were able to cope with the rhinoceroses and ultimately to return and cultivate the flat ground.

This story raises the whole question of how much value is to be attached to native tales. Sometimes they seem to be pure inventions, "philosophic myths," made up to explain what the Kaffir does not know. But I am inclined to think that this story may be genuine; and it is apparently true, as the same correspondent states, that there are fertile plains in the northern part of Mashonaland which are infested by rhinoceroses and where no villages are to be found. However, the native story, though it may be genuine, and though it might explain the low walls in some parts of the country, will not explain the high walls, still less the forts of such a site as the Niekerk Ruins. As to that site, I cannot consider it reasonably probable that any but the lowest tiers of walls were built for purposes of cultivation, and even these are not best explained by that view.

Note 5.—**Respect paid to Mountains. Burial.**—It is difficult to avoid the impression that the position of this place of offerings just under the great mountain is in some way significant. The mediæval Kaffirs, like some of the present day, used to bury their chiefs on mountains. So Dos Santos (*T.R.* vii. 196) says, "Every year in the month of September, when the new moon appears, Quiteve ascends a very high mountain situated near the city called Zimbaoe, in which he dwells, on the summit of which he performs grand obsequies for the kings, his predecessors, who are all buried there." Similarly the kings of Quissanga were buried in a cave on a mountain (*T.R.* vii. 378, and cf. vii. 381). I had not the opportunity thoroughly to explore the great mountain at the Niekerk Ruins, but would recommend it as worth while for any other person who may go there to investigate.

With regard to burial customs in general, I doubt whether any cemetery will be found amongst the Rhodesian ruins. It is very possible that only the chiefs were actually buried. Negroes, even when not cannibals, have curious ways of disposing of their dead. We read, indeed, of the common people of Quiteve burying in their own houses (*T.R.* vii. 278), and of other Kaffirs burying in the forest (*T.R.* vii. 213, 265). But some kept the bones of their dead "as in a garden" (*T.R.* vi. 269), and the characteristic attitude of savages is well expressed in another passage (*T.R.* ii. 143), where it is stated that "no one knows when one of them dies, nor is his place of burial made known except to his parents, children, brothers and sisters, or nearest relations."

Note 6.—**Portuguese References to Ruins North of Inyanga.**—Apart from the passages mentioned in Note 16, which seem to refer rather to the neighbourhood of the Zimbabwe near Victoria, there are three in which Portuguese writers speak of stone ruins in a district between the Zambesi and Inyanga, viz., the part about Mount Afur.

Manuel da Faria e Sousa, a seventeenth-century author, says, "In the mountain Afur near Masapa are seen the ruins of stately buildings supposed to be palaces and castles" (*T.R.* i. 23).

Dos Santos (1609) states of Mount "Fura" that "on the summit of this mountain some fragments of old walls and ancient ruins of stone and mortar are still standing, which clearly show that once there were houses here and strong dwellings, which are not to be found in all Kaffraria, as even the king's palaces are built of wood covered with clay and thatched with straw" (*T.R.* vii. 275).

Diogo de Couto (born 1542, died 1616) believed, like Dos Santos, that the Queen of Sheba took her gold from these parts—a belief which it was quite proper for a *mediæval* historian to hold. He writes (*T.R.* vi. 391 and vi. 337, 338), "Even at the present day in those parts, at the markets of

APPENDIX II—NOTES

Masapa and Nabertura, there are great stone edifices which she commanded to be built for herself, which are called Simbaoe by the Kaffirs, and which are like strong bulwarks. These the Kaffirs always consider to be the means by which Monomotapa obtained dominion over all Kaffraria."

I must confess to appreciating the native tradition preserved in this last sentence considerably more than De Couto's own theories on biblical archæology. In Note 16 there will be occasion to refer to that passage of De Goes which suggests that places like the Great Zimbabwe were inhabited by Kaffirs in the sixteenth century. And that Dos Santos was not justified in his assertion that no stone buildings were constructed in "Kaffraria" in mediæval times is proved by the statement of Alcaçova (1506) that in the city of "Mokomba Menamotapam" the "houses of the king were of stone and clay, very large" (*T.R.* i. 65 and i. 59).

Note 7.—**Handcuffs.**—A pair of exactly the same form as that from Dhlo-Dhlo may be seen represented on a Valencia tile of the sixteenth century.

Note 8.—**Copper-working by Natives.**—Dos Santos writes (*T.R.* vii. 380), "Copper is taken from the mines with the earth, and by being melted is soon separated; it is then again melted and cast into any shape wished by making holes in the earth." He also mentions (*T.R.* vii. 270) that "copper bars about half a span in length and two fingers wide" were used as money on the Zambesi.

Another author (*T.R.* iii. 505) states that ingots in the form of "two Saint Andrew's crosses joined together by a bar in the middle" were used as money in the same region. To the manufacture of copper bracelets by the natives there are several references (*T.R.* iii. 229, 416; vii. 285).

Note 9.—**Pin in Form of Maltese Cross.**—There is a curious passage in Manuel de Faria e Sousa which may have a bearing on the origin of this ornament. He says, "King John was informed by the Benin ambassador, who came to desire that priests should be sent to them, that two hundred and fifty leagues beyond them was the most powerful prince of all those countries, called Ogane, by whom the kings of Benin for their security were confirmed, receiving of him a staff with a head and cross like that of Malta, all of brass curiously wrought" (*T.R.* i. 1).

In this connection it may be remarked in passing that the wooden platter carved with bungled figures of the zodiac, which has been so often reproduced (and is now at Groote Schuur), belongs to a class quite well known to ethnographers as coming from the west coast of Africa. It is of course not Oriental, but Kaffir work influenced by European.

The iron bells found by Mr. R. N. Hall at Zimbabwe are also of a kind well known on the west coast of Africa.

Note 10.—**Incised Patterns on Pottery.**—The geometrical patterns on the pottery from the Niekerk Ruins, and on that from Zimbabwe, were incised with a pointed stick while the clay was still wet. But the lines and cross-hatchings on some of the painted pottery from Dhlo-Dhlo and Khami were engraved after the clay had already been baked. This was done in all probability with a stone flake, as has been discovered by Mr. Henry Balfour, who further suggests that in this practice may be found an explanation of the fact that at Dhlo-Dhlo and Khami untrimmed flakes preponderate enormously in number over any other kind of stone implement (see his article in *Man*, Feb. 1906).

Note 11.—**The Portuguese Search after Silver Mines.**—Manuel de Faria e Sousa (*T.R.* i. 38) assigns to the year 1616 the famous treaty by which the "Emperor of Monomotapa," in return for Portuguese aid against his rebellious vassal Chunzo, "gave all his mines to the king of Portugal, making a resignation of them to Diogo Simoens Madera, commander of Tete, who was then in his service." By this instrument the Monomotapa, as we learn, ceded "all his mines of gold, silver, copper, tin, iron, and lead." Bocarro, who quotes the document in full (*T.R.* iii. 368), states its date as 1607, and gives the name of the then Monomotapa as Gasse Lucere. The Portuguese fondly thought that this treaty would lead to the realisation of the hopes which had prompted the ill-starred expedition of Francisco Barrets (*T.R.* iii. 251, 253; vii. 283, 285, etc.). It would seem that a similar formal donation was made again about a century later by another Monomotapa, Dom Pedro, a convert of the Dominicans (*T.R.* v. 71).

But the search after silver mines was doomed to be fruitless. According to Bocarro, silver was actually discovered by Diogo Simões de Madera in the territory of Chicova, eight days' journey from Tete, but owing to the persecutions of the judge, Francisco de Fonseca Pinto, the work there was abandoned (*T.R.* iii. 387-435, and cf. i. 40-44). The official report on this expedition, moreover, prepared by the Governor-General of Goa in 1619 for the Viceroy, states that there is no doubt that Simões de Madera discovered silver at the place mentioned, but refuses to decide whether it was merely buried treasure or the genuine output from mines (*T.R.* iv. 155-162). And it would seem that the doubt was never settled, and that in spite of much correspondence no serious search for the mines was ever again made. In the year 1640 the king of Portugal complains (*T.R.* iv. 287) that there is still no certainty as to the existence of the silver mines. In 1719 another expedition was commanded from Lisbon (*T.R.* v. 53), but there is no record that it was ever carried out.

The supposed localities of several silver mines are given by Bocarro (*T.R.* iii. 415).

Note 12.—**Tin.**—"Tin" is included among the minerals of which the mines were ceded to Portugal by the treaty referred to in the last note. Theal does not give the Spanish original from which he translates the account given by Manuel de Faria e Sousa, but presumably the word used is "estaño," which would be correctly translated "tin." Bocarro uses the corresponding Portuguese word "estanho," and I think that Theal should have rendered it *tin* rather than *pewter* in his translation of Bocarro's version of the treaty (*T.R.* iii. 368).

In other passages there is a certain ambiguity. There are three in which mention is made of a metal which is either tin or pewter, and which was used in the form of money or for making ornaments. Thus (*T.R.* iii. 229 and 180) the natives make their hair grow long by fastening to the ends of the locks "pedacinhos de cobre ou calaim"; and (*T.R.* iii. 235 and 185) have "muito ferro e cobre, e calaim de que usaõ muito os naturaes fazerem suas joyas e cousinhas muitas." And in *T.R.* iii. 505 and 499 we read of square plaques of this metal being used in barter—"Do calaim uzaõ em premutaçaõ, como moeda quadrada em huã das faces como pontas de diamante, que recebem da fundiçao." But an analogous passage in Dos Santos (*T.R.* vii. 270) states explicitly that these plaques were *tin*—"Tambem e moeda corrente estanho, a que chamam calaim, feito em pães, cada pão de meio arratel."

Note 13.—**Beads and other Articles of Barter.**—Beads are constantly mentioned by the Portuguese writers as being articles of barter in their African possessions. The most famous were the "Cambay beads" (*T.R.* i. 94, 104; ii. 26), which were made at various places in India (*T.R.* iii. 234, 303). The natives threaded them on fibre and worked them up into necklaces, etc., just as they work up the beads imported at the present day (*T.R.* iii. 235; vi. 368).

Besides these were imported transparent glass beads in large quantities. It is not stated where they were manufactured; they are mentioned in lists which include both Indian and European products (*T.R.* ii. 26, 31). It is noteworthy that all glass-work, amongst which glass beads are specifically included, was excepted from the free-trading ordinance of 1755, and reserved as a crown monopoly (*T.R.* v. 224, 229; ix. 106).

The articles of barter are detailed in various passages. The principal were cloth and beads, but there are also mentioned needles, pins, knives, looking-glasses, candles, soap, zafran, pepper, silks, calico, macassars, dimity, linen, tin, caps, trappings of hawks, little bells from Flanders, rattles, corals, iron articles (*T.R.* i. 41, 94, 104; ii. 26, 31, 35, 46, 405; iii. 235).

The chief source from which the imported articles were obtained was India, and at the beginning of the sixteenth century the negroes of Sofala would not accept European goods, but insisted on having "articles which the Moors procured from India, especially from Cambaya" (*T.R.* vi. 277; cf. vi. 258). Thus Pedro da Nhaya was sent on one occasion from Sofala to Melinde expressly to obtain Indian goods which the "Moors" had procured (*T.R.* ii. 33).

The Portuguese did not themselves take these articles of barter far up country; at first they probably employed Arab intermediaries. But soon they refused to tolerate the pressure of these dangerous rivals, and brought pressure to bear on the native chiefs to expel all "Moors" from the country (*T.R.* iii. 155, 247, 251; v. 291, etc.); and in the seventeenth century it is stated that "all the trade and merchandise of the Portuguese in these extensive territories passes through the hands of Kaffirs, either their captives or individuals known to them, to whom they entrust large quantities of the goods most esteemed and valuable among them, which they carry for many leagues into the interior and barter for gold and ivory, returning punctually with all the gain . . ." (*T.R.* ii. 418).

Note 14.—**The Place called Zimbaoe by the Portuguese.**—The word "Zimbaoe," as I have said in the text, is simply a synonym for the capital of a chief. Accordingly it is applied by the Portuguese writers to the capital of other chiefs besides the Monomotapa; the principal place of the Quiteve, for instance, is several times so called (*T.R.* i. 29; vi. 388; vii. 185, 378).

Monclaro, writing of the expedition of Francisco Barreto in 1569, an expedition in which he himself played so inglorious a part, locates the court of the Monomotapa "which they call Zimbaoe" near Masapa (*T.R.* iii. 237); and this is the place which is generally meant by all the writers after the middle of the sixteenth century. It was here, that is to say, a little north of the Afur district, that the Monomotapa then had his capital. If there are any remains of it left it may not be impossible to find it; for there are various indications of distance and direction, which, in spite of discrepancies, may serve to indicate the site. The chief guide is that it stood near Masapa, which can be approximately located by the references given above in my Note 3; and that it was only three days' journey from Chicova, which is described as being 24 leagues by land + 20 leagues by river westward of Tete (*T.R.* iii. 403, 406, and cf. 467. Also see ii. 438; iii. 482).

Note 15.—**The "Empire" of the Monomotapa.**—The character and extent of the Monomotapan rule have been the subject of considerable dispute. Some writers have even gone so far as to represent that rule as being a mere fiction on the part of the Portuguese; who were, of course, interested in exaggerating it as being the basis of their claim to the ownership of certain territories. It is natural that the most extreme version should be that which was put forward in the controversy about Delagoa Bay, when it was asserted on behalf of the crown of Portugal that "the king of Monomotapa" in 1629 had ceded his dominions which "extended beyond this bay and nearly up to the Cape of Good Hope" (*T.R.* ix. 181).

This statement as to the original extent of the dominions was not wholly without support in the historians, for De Goes in 1566 had written that "in the interior of this land of Sofala, and commencing nearly from the Cape of Good Hope, lies the great kingdom of Benomotapa" (*T.R.* iii. 128). But the more moderate and usual view is represented by Diogo de Couto in 1616, who speaks of the Monomotapa—(the word is a dynastic title and not the name of a country)—as having "obtained dominion over all Kaffraria from the Cabo das Correntes to the great river Zambesi" (*T.R.* vi. 391).

The Portuguese writers are unanimous in describing the Monomotapa as a powerful lord with many chiefs subject to him. No doubt it was an error to translate his title as "emperor," but the misconception was probably no greater than that of the historians who have ascribed a similar power and position to the Mexican Montezuma. In treating of the Mohammedan colonies along the East Coast, the Portuguese historians similarly term their rulers "kings"; which is no doubt an exaggeration, but quite pardonable inasmuch as the persons referred to were unquestionably sheikhs of some importance.

I think, therefore, that it is unreasonable scepticism which doubts the predominance over a large region south of the Zambesi, at any rate in the sixteenth century, of a great chief who was called the Monomotapa. It is possible that he did not always belong to the same tribe or section of a tribe;

and it is worth noting that at the beginning of the sixteenth century a Monomotapa bore the name of "Mokomba," and a century later another was called "Mambo" (*T.R.* i. 64 ; vii. 288). He is usually described as ruling over "Mocaranga" or "the Mocarangas" in general (*T.R.* i. 397 ; ii. 66, 414 ; iii. 358, 482 ; vi. 391 ; vii. 273). The extent of his territory varied ; as it existed in the seventeenth century it is described by several writers (*T.R.* i. 22, 23 ; iii. 355, 356 ; vii. 273).

By the seventeenth century, however, the paramountcy of the Monomotapa seems to have been greatly impaired in consequence of rebellions detailed by Dos Santos and others (*T.R.* vii. 273 ; and cf. *T.R.* i. 64 ; iv. 277). His residence (his Zimbabwe) was then near the Zambesi, and a Portuguese garrison was maintained in it. From 1607 onwards he was generally the puppet or at least the nominee of the Portuguese. The title seems to have disappeared by the beginning of the nineteenth century (*T.R.* vii. 377).

Other references than these given above are *T.R.* i. 15, 23, 80, 82, 95, 395, 401, 403 ; ii. 36, 362, 438, 445 ; iii. 227, 353-356, 367, 395 ; v. 72 ; vi. 264, 270 ; ix. 151. And with regard to the Mocarangas see *T.R.* i. 24 ; ii. 66, 413, 414 ; iii. 358, 482 ; vi. 391.

Note 16.—**Portuguese References to a Building like the "Elliptical Temple."**—The account which De Goes gives of a building like the "Elliptical Temple" at Zimbabwe near Victoria is worth quoting in full in the original language, so that the exact context and meaning may be appreciated. It runs as follows :—" O Rei desta prouincia he grãde senhor porq̃ segundo dizem, tem em circuito seus senhorios mais doito cētas legoas, afora algũs Reis, & senhores q̃ lhe obedecem, & pagam tributo douro, do qual ja os da terra tomarão o gosto que lhe os mouros q̃ antrelles viuem, deram de muito tempo a esta parte, & lhe nos acrecentamos, em quasi setenta annos q̃ a q̃ descobrimos estas prouincias. Todo este regno de Benomotapa he muito fertil de mantimentos, fruitas, & criações, a nella tantos Elephantes brauos, q̃ se nam passa anno nenhum, em q̃ não matem os q̃ os caçam de quatro a cinco mil de q̃ vai perà India grãde soma de marfim. He mui abundante douro, o qual se acha em grande cantidade, assi em minas, como em rios, & alagoas : destas minas ahi hũas no regno de Batua, de q̃ o Rei he vassalo do de Benomotapa, a comarca em q̃ estam se chama Toro a toda em campo raso, & sam as mais antiguas q̃ se sabem em toda aquella regiã. No meo desta campina esta hũa fortaleza, toda laurada de cantaria muito grossa, & grande, pela banda de fora, & de dentro, de obra muito prima, & bem assentada, tanto q̃ segundo dizem,

APPENDIX II—NOTES

se não enxerga cal nas junturas della : sobella porta desta fortaleza esta hũ litreiro talhado em pedra, q̃ por muito antigo se não entende o q̃ quer dizer. E em algũs comaros que aquella campina faz, estão outras fortalezas feitas do mesmo modo, nas quaes todas tem el Rei capitães, & o q̃ se pode dellas julgar he, que forã feitas para guarda daquellas minas douro, & receber o Principe q̃ as mandou fazer alli o direito, q̃ lhe delle pagauão, per officiaes q̃ pera isso nellas teria, por q̃ assi o fazem ao presente os Reis daquelle regno de Benomotapa, do qual os habitadores sam todos pretos de cabello frisado" . . . (*T.R.* iii. 55 ; translated in *T.R.* iii. 129).

There is not a word of the Queen of Sheba or Solomon's mines in this admirably straightforward account. It should be noted that the writer does not pretend to have seen or visited the buildings, he describes them from *report* only, like De Barros, who derived his information from some "Moors" who had seen them, and who said that it had not been erected by "Moors" (*T.R.* vi. 268). This explains such misstatements as that the building was square and that it had an inscription. No doubt it was the chevron ornamentation which was mistaken for an inscription.

There are only two other references to ruins which I know. The first is Bocarro's statement that "there is also another kingdom adjoining the Mokaranga, which is the kingdom of Beza, where there is a palace of the ancient monomotapas, which the Kaffirs hold to be a supreme piece of work. All the monomotapas are buried there and it serves them as a cemetery" (*T.R.* iii. 356 and 266-267). The other is a single sentence in Manuel de Faria e Sousa, viz. : "Here" (apparently 150 leagues from Sofala) "are some buildings of wonderful structure with inscriptions of unknown characters, but the natives know nothing of their foundations" (*T.R.* i. 15). So that including the references quoted in Note 6 there are only seven passages in all the Portuguese records which make mention of any stone ruins in any part of the country. This would be most remarkable, if it could be supposed that the Portuguese had penetrated far or were acquainted at first hand with the interior. But those who have studied the history will have appreciated the fact that the Portuguese knew very little except the coast and the country immediately bordering on the Zambesi. The part which they held most effectively was the line of the Zambesi, from its mouth to a little beyond Tete. They knew something of the country just south of the river, and had established a garrison at Masapa (cf. Note 3), nearly as far to the south as the Afur district, but that was their farthest limit. So that when a writer like Dos Santos make wide generalisations about "all Kaffraria" his statements must be received with caution. And when Monclaro (*T.R.* iii. 231) says of the natives about the Zambesi that they have "never raised a stone upon a stone to build a house or wall; their only houses are small straw huts plastered with clay, resembling round dove-cotes," he may be describing correctly the particular places in which he had travelled, but there is no justification for extending his statements to include regions in the interior which he had never seen. I have remarked already (Note 6) that the assertion that the mediæval Kaffirs never built in stone is controverted by Alcaçova's mention of the houses of the Monomotapa being of *stone* and clay.

Note 17.—**Religion of the Builders of Zimbabwe, etc.**—As I have stated in the text, there is no sufficient reason for supposing the great tower at Zimbabwe to be the symbol of phallic worship, and there are some good reasons for rejecting any such theory. There has been much confusion of thought amongst the writers who have treated of this supposed form of primitive religion. In the first place, it is misleading to describe as "phallic worship" these rites in which an anthropomorphic deity of any kind appears; the cults of various Egyptian and Indian deities, and all observances of the class described in Frazer's *Golden Bough* belong to this category. Secondly, if there is any evidence of actual worship of the phallus in any part of the world it is to be found amongst the most typical of all negroes, viz. those of the West Coast of Africa (see Ellis, *Ewe-speaking Peoples*). But to treat such observance sas criteria of race is, in my opinion, utterly unscientific.

A few hints may be obtained from the Portuguese writers as to what the religion of the East Coast negroes really was in their day. Such general statements as that they "made no idols" and "believed in one God" need not be too implicitly believed; they belong to a class of assertions familiar enough to all who have tried to obtain information on such subjects (see also *T.R.* vi. 269 for a contradiction of them). But when small details are given they may be considered to have genuine value. Thus in *T.R.* i. 24 there is the statement that "they believe their kings go to heaven and call them Muzimos, and call upon them in the time of need, as we on the saints (cf. *T.R.* vii. 295); in the same place (*T.R.* i. 24) mention is made of human sacrifice (cf. *T.R.* iii. 361) and of feasts at the time of new moon (cf. *T.R.* vii. 196). From *T.R.* i. 27; ii. 93, 144, 147; iii. 129, etc., we learn of their belief in witches and wizards. In *T.R.* i. 401 there is what looks like an allusion to stone-worship. But the main

APPENDIX II—NOTES

feature of their religion was evidently ancestor-worship (see *T.R.* i. 24 ; iii. 359, 399 ; vii. 196, 199, 265).

Note 18.—**Gold-working by Natives in Mediæval Times.**—The native processes of gold-working are described by the Portuguese writers in several passages. The natives are said (*T.R.* iii. 234) to have "a great love of gold, and make different things of it which they wear round their necks like beads, and also use it in trading for cloth." But their methods were rudimentary, for in the same place we read —" When the Monomotapa wants gold he sends a cow to those of his people who are to dig, and it is divided among them according to their labour and the number of days they are required to work ; each one extracts at the most a cruzado or a cruzado and a half a day." In *T.R.* iii. 489, 490 there is a detailed account of the way in which the Kaffirs worked the 'marondos" or holes in which they dug the gold, but it is too long to quote, in this place. Dos Santos describes (*T.R.* vii. 218) three native methods of extracting and collecting gold, viz. "the first and most usual manner" by making "deep holes and mines" ; the second, which is practised when it rains, for then the Kaffirs seek it in all the springs of the mountains and plains, when it is laid bare by the torrents and currents of water" ; the third when "the gold is extracted from certain stones which are found in particular mines." It is worth observing that Dos Santos says "This gold from the stones is called by the Kaffirs *matuca* ; it is inferior and of few carats fineness. All the other gold they call *dahabo*, whether it be in powder or in pieces." *Dahabo* is, of course the regular Arabic word *dahab*.

Reference has been made in the text to the Monomotapa sending gold beads as a present ; so again in *T.R.* ii. 27, 30, we read how the king of Sofala made the Portuguese captain presents of gold beads threaded together. In *T.R.* i. 94 is Duarte Barbosa's well-known account of the trade in the early sixteenth century between the "Moors" of Sofala and the "heathens of the kingdom of Benametapa"; the Arabs brought Indian products for which they received gold by weight.

Note 19.—**Localities and Dating of Gold Mines.**—The localities of the gold mines known to the Portuguese are given in the following passages : *T.R.* i. 15, 21, 23, 29, 63 ; ii. 416 ; iii. 227, 233, 487-492 ; iv. 35, 160, 278 ; vi. 266, 367, 389 ; vii. 185, 218, 276, 280. But it will be difficult to identify them until a more exact study has been made of the comparative topography in the Portuguese writers. It would seem that the mines of Manica were those from which the Portuguese drew the most.

As to the general question of the antiquity of the gold mines in Rhodesia, there can from the nature of the case, be little direct evidence. So few objects are found in the old workings, that the archæologist has no material on which to base a judgment. It was my work to decide the date of the *ruins*, not of the mines, and I cannot dogmatise about the latter. I may, however, point out that the documents prove *some* of the gold mines to be mediæval inasmuch as they were worked by Kaffirs in the time of the Portuguese and mediæval Arabs; and I have already suggested that the probabilities are strongly against any settlements having been made on East Africa from over seas before the eleventh century. Up to the present moment it has not been possible to adduce any evidence that the gold mines were worked by any people but the Kaffirs, and the *onus probandi* therefore lies with those who maintain them to be ancient.

It is sometimes stated that the mere quantity of gold extracted from the land proves very many centuries of exploitation. But it is difficult to obtain an estimate that can be trusted to be even roughly correct. Nor do we know at all how much activity was displayed in working the mines during the few centuries preceding the Portuguese colonisation. It may be worth noting that in 1506, Alcaçova states the annual export from Sofala to vary from a sum equivalent to about £109,000 sterling, to a sum equivalent to £141,600. This was exclusive of the leakage to the Moors through Angoya (see *T.R.* i. 66).

Note 20.—**That the Monomotapa was a negro** in the seventeenth century is proved by the statement in *T.R.* i. 24 that he was a Mocaranga; as well as by the passage referred to in the text (*T.R.* i. 401 and 375). There is not the slightest hint in any of the Portuguese writings that the rulers of the Monomotapan state or states were of a different race from their subjects. Duarte Barbosa at the very beginning of the sixteenth century says that the "great kingdom of Benametapa is "peopled by heathens whom the Moors call Kaffirs; they are black men." And Dos Santos, a century later, describes the Quiteve as "a woolly-haired Kaffir" (*T.R.* vii. 190) and compare (cf. *T.R.* v. 37).

Note 21.—**Devastating Hordes in South and Central Africa**.—As illustrating the way in which these parts of Africa had been devastated time after time, even before the advent of the Zulus, I may refer to several passages in the Portuguese histories. Thus (*T.R.* i. 31), in the year 1570, "there came upon the country of Mozambique such an inundation of Kaffirs that they

APPENDIX II—NOTES

could not be numbered. They came from that part of Monomotapa where is the great lake out of which spring these great rivers whose source was formerly unknown. . . . They left no other signs of the towns they passed by, but the heaps of ruins and bones of the inhabitants" (see also *T.R.* vi. 392). About twenty years later took place the famous raid of the Zimbas or Muzimbas (*T.R.* i. 384, etc.), "a strange people never before seen there, who, leaving their own country, traversed a great part of this Ethiopia, like a scourge of God, destroying every living thing they came across with a brutality greater than that of wild beasts." These Zimbas, who were cannibals, marched 20,000 strong, taking no women or children with them. Again we may read (*T.R.* iv. 50) how in the year 1602 "a horde of people from the interior called Cabires, who eat human flesh, is entering the kingdom of Monomotapa, and this king being weak, is in great terror." Similarly, in 1823, Captain Owen, writing of the natives about Delagoa Bay, says (*T.R.* ii. 469) that on the western bank of King George "are now settled the Vatwahs, who have lately overrun and destroyed many of the neighbouring countries."

It seems extremely probable that the builders of the Rhodesian ruins may have succumbed to some such invasion, perhaps unrecorded, as these that have been mentioned.

Note 22.—**Portuguese Influence at Penhalanga.**—From Umtali itself no evidence of Portuguese trade has been obtained, but it must be remembered that the site has not as yet been extensively explored. On the other hand, there is evidence of Portuguese influence as close to Umtali as Penhalanga. Some clay crucibles found near the "Castle Rocks" were submitted to Prof. W. Gowland for examination. His report is contained in the *Proceedings of the Society of Antiquaries* for 9th March 1905. The crucibles look very primitive in form, but were found to "differ both in shape and in the manner in which they have been used from those of prehistoric or early historic times." . . . "The crucibles can only have been used for casting small ornaments and other objects, and not for the extraction of metal from ore." Their contents proved the date at which they had been used. Crucible No. 1 "contained a few very small granules of a copper-zinc-tin alloy"; Nos. 2, 3, 4 "contained a few minute granules of copper." The copper granules contained 99.65 of copper; "the metal was tough and of much greater purity than it would have been if it had been obtained by a native process." "The presence of so much zinc (13.68) in the copper-zinc-tin alloy, which is really a crude brass, indicates a comparatively recent date for the crucibles. The original alloy could not have been made locally, or in early times, as the natives could not have been acquainted with the metal zinc." . . . "The source from which it was derived was doubtless the copper and brass penannular rings worn as ornaments for the arms or legs, which were imported by the Portuguese into their African settlements for use in barter." "The alloy contains practically the same percentage of zinc as some of the ornamental castings from Benin, which had a similar origin."

The fragment of stoneware—it should perhaps rather be styled "porcelain"—from Umtali is covered with a celadon glaze which definitely dates it to the thirteenth to fifteenth centuries A.D.

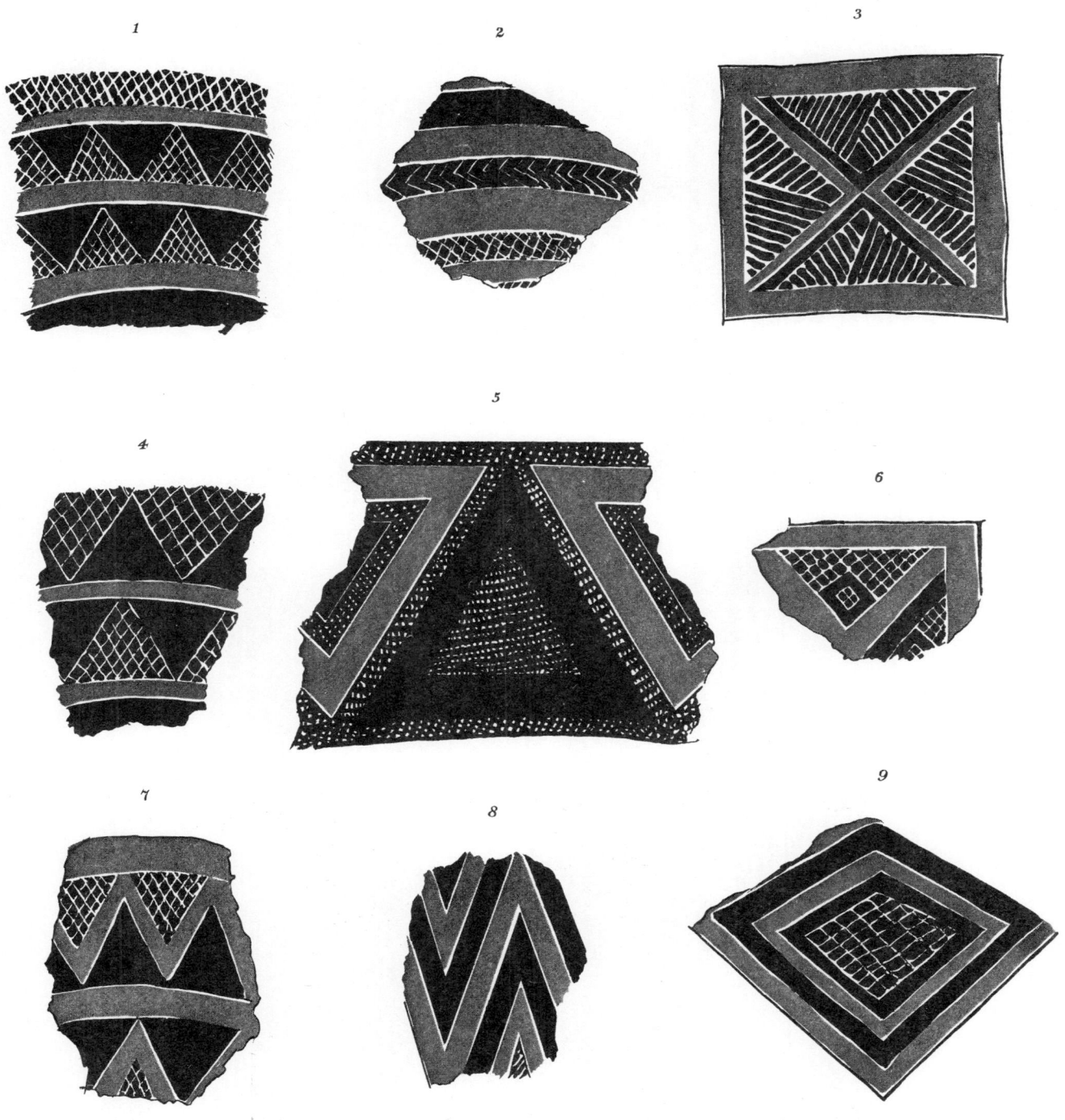

PAINTED POTTERY FROM DHLO-DHLO.

PLATE XXXIV.

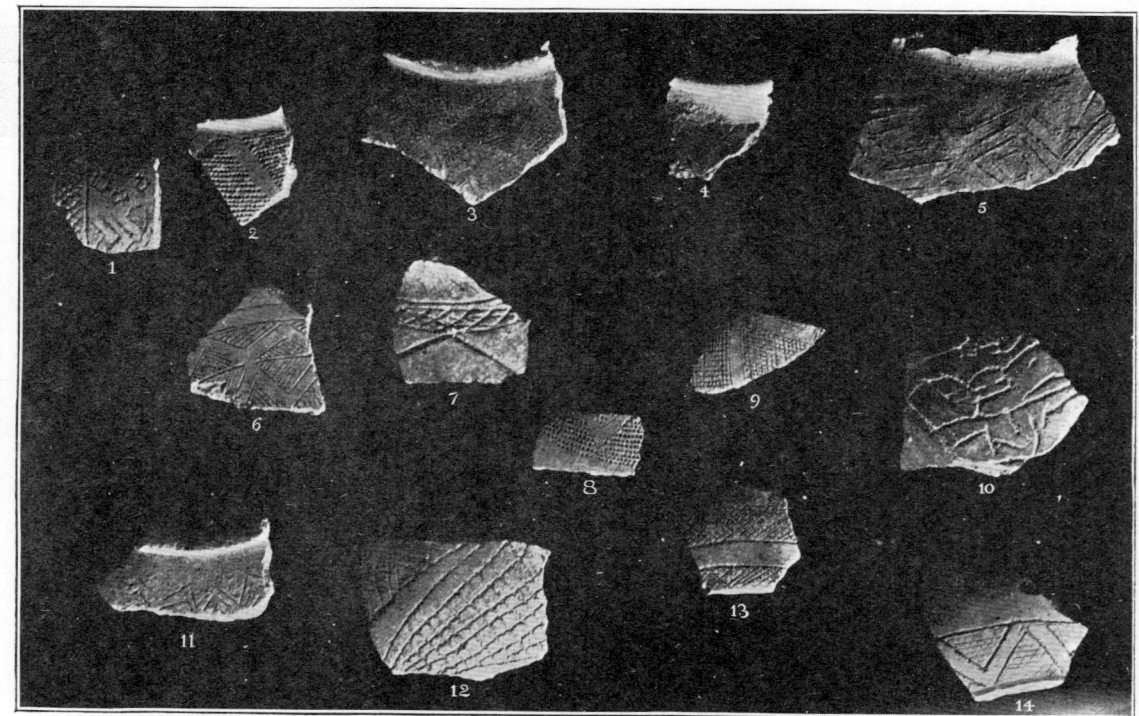

POTTERY FROM DHLO-DHLO.　　　　　See page 46.

POTTERY FROM KHAMI.　　　　　See page 58.

PLATE XXXV.

POTTERY FROM ZIMBABWE.   *See page* 81.

POTTERY FROM KHAMI.   *See page* 58.

POTTERY FROM ZIMBABWE.   *See page* 81.

PLATE XXXVI.

(a) STREAM AND IRRIGATION FURROW, INYANGA.

See page 12.

(b) MODERN HUT AND GRAIN-SHELTER NEAR ZIMBABWE.

INDEX

Acropolis, 76
Adze, 22
Alloy, 103
Altar, 17, 22, 35, 70, 71, 78
Amulet, 33, 58
Animal pottery figures, 33, 36, 58, 81
Antelope teeth, 33
Arab glass, 64, 82; influence, 1; silver work, 81
Arrow, 10, 17, 33, 58
Ash heap, 44
Awl, bone, 33
Axe, 19, 30, 33, 43, 58

Banquette, 4, 5, 6, 24
Bar, entrance, 18, 21, 24
Barter, 95
Baulk, 41, 43, 56, 65
Beads, 43, 46, 80, 82, 95; glass, 82; glaze, 46, 49; gold, 75; ivory, 33, 45; porcelain, 46; shell, 45, 49; steatite, 33. See also Cambay
Bearings, compass, 23
Bell metal, 45
Bells, 94
Bibliography, 90
Bones, 10, 17, 27, 28, 30, 58
Boulders, carved, 36
Bracelet, 33, 43, 45, 58, 78
Bronze, 11, 22, 45, 49, 58, 78
Building, methods of, 4, 5, 6, 9, 10, 15, 18, 26, 36, 39, 41, 52, 67, 76, 84
Buildings, types of, 18, 20, 24, 26, 28, 37, 39, 64, 83
Burial, 28, 92

Cairn, 31
Cambay beads, 49, 95
Cannon, bronze, 50
Carvings, 35
Celadon glaze, 82
Cement, 42, 44, 54, 62, 64, 84; covering, 66, 76
Charcoal, 19, 27, 31, 66
China, Nankin, 43, 47, 63, 80, 81
Chisel, 58
Citadel, 39, 43, 55. See Pit-dwelling
Clay, burned, 27
Colonies, E. African, 1
Compartments, 7, 8, 9, 18, 21, 42, 53, 56, 57, 71
Conclusions, 11, 28, 37, 46, 63, 83 *sq.*
Conical tower, 73
Copper, 22, 33, 36, 43, 45, 49, 55, 58, 67, 78, 103; pattern on, 22; working by natives, 93

Corridor, 7, 9, 17, 29
Crucibles, 103
Cylinder, masonry, 76

De Battos, 60
Debris heap, 32, 44
De Goes, 98
Dhlo-Dhlo, 38 *sq.*, 84, 86
Dish, 82
Door-post, 53
Dos Santos, 92 *sq.*

Emblems, tribal, 76, 78
Enamel, 45, 49, 58, 79
Enclosure, 7, 8, 17, 22, 40, etc.
Entrance, 4, 7, 18, 20, 24, 41, 52, 55, 71, 76
Erosion, 30, 57, 63, 78, 87
Excavations, results of, 10, 31, 42, 45; methods, 32; at Zimbabwe, 88. See also Objects

Faience, 80, 81
Feast, ceremonial, 32
Figurine pottery. See Animal
Fort, 4 *sq.*, 24, 38, 55, 69; Portuguese, 91. See also Citadel
Fuba stones, 36

Geometrical patterns. See Pottery
Glass, 43, 63, 80, 82
Glaze on metal, 79; on pottery, 36, 46, 58, 62, 80, 82
Gold mines, 101; wire, 45, 49, 78; working, 75, 101
Gowland, Prof., 79, 103
Granary, 44
Grinding stones, 17, 19, 21, 27, 44
Guillain, 90

Hall, Mr. R. N., 61
Hand cuffs, 45, 93
Hill forts, 4 *sq.*, 24, 25, 38, 55
Human remains, 28
Huts, 19, 26, 27, 42, 51, 53, 54, 57, 61, 64; walls, of, 27; chief's, 51, 53, 71

Incised patterns, 22, 33, 46, 58, 81, 94
Invasions of S. Africa, 1, 103
Inyanga, 3 *sq.*, 86, 87; walls at, 91; ruins north of, 92
Iron objects found, 10, 17, 19, 20, 21, 25, 27, 33, 36, 43, 45, 55, 58, 79, 80, 88, 89
Irrigation trenches, 6, 12, 28*n*

Ivory, 33, 58. See Beads

Key, 58
Khami, 55 *sq.*, 85
Kilwa, chronicle of, 1

Lintel, 7, 9, 21, 25; wanting, 41, 76
Loophole, 4, 7, 91

Mæander pattern, 33
Maltese Cross, pin in form of, 93
Monoliths, 69, 74, 77, 78
Monomotapa, 48, 59, 97; race of, 85, 102
Mountain, cult on, 92
Myth, ætiological, 91

Nail, 54
Nanatali, 41, 51, 86
Needle, 58
Niekerk, 14 *sq.*, 87; Division I. 25; Division II. 22, 26; Division VI. 16

Objects found, 10, 25, 27, 33, 43, 44 *sq.*, 57, 58, 63, 78. See also Excavations, Pottery, Iron, Bones, etc.
Offerings, place of, 31
Origin of buildings, 28, 37

Passage, parallel, 26, 72
Patterns. See Copper, Incised, Mæander, Pottery, Walls
Paving-slabs, 19
Periplus, 1
Persian Faience, 81; inscription, 80
Phalli, 73, 81
Phallic worship, 73, 100
Philips Ruins, 76
Pigments, 49, 50, 58
Pin in form of Maltese Cross, 45, 48, 93
Pingstone, Mr. G. A., 78
Pipe, 55, 58
Pit-dwelling, 5, 6, 7, 11, 16, 22, 27; modifications of, 20, 24, 29, 36
Platform, 8, 10, 25, 39, 41, 51, 61, 69
Plumbago varnish, 81
Porcelain, 81, 89, 104. See also China, Stoneware
Portuguese influence, 86, 91, 103; authors, 92
Pottery, 10, 11, 17, 22, 30, 32, 43, 46, 49, 55, 57, 58, 61, 81, 88, 89; patterns on, 17, 22, 33, 46, 58, 81, 94

Quartz arrow heads, 17, 33

Read, Mr. C. H., 80, 81
Religion of builders of Zimbabwe, 100
Ribbon, bronze, 79

Silver pin, 45, 48, 93 ; mines, 48, 94 ; work, 81
Slab, 17, 43
Smelting-place, 43
Soapstone, 22, 35 sq., 55, 58, 76, 81
Sofala, 86
Spear-heads, 55, 58, 89
Spindle-whorl, 43, 61, 81, 88
Spoon, 43
Steps, 62, 64, 76
Stone implements, 33, 45, 58. See Axe, Arrow

Stoneware, 36, 58, 63, 80, 87
Strandes, 90
Strigil, 22
Subterranean corridor. See Corridor

Teeth, 33
"Temple, Elliptical," 61, 67 sq., 98 ; age of, 63 ; plan of, 70
Terraces, 15, 20. See also Walls
Theal, G. M., 90
Tin slag, 43, 49, 58, 77, 95
Towers, round, 69
Treasure pit, 53

Umtali, 2, 35 sq., 86

Vase in form of animal, 33
Venetian bead, 82

Walls, concentric, 15, 39 ; decoration of, 39, 51, 52, 55, 56, 69, 74 ; height of, 9, 10, 16, 21, 39 ; in tiers, 39, 52, 55
Wheel-made pottery, 55
White, Mr. Franklin, 40
Wire, copper, 33, 36, 43, 45, 49, 55, 58, 61 ; bronze, 45 ; gold, 45, 49, 78, 79 ; iron, 36, 79, 81

Zimbabwe, 59 sq., 84 ; Temple, 61, 67, 98 ; valley ruins, 75 ; acropolis, 75, 76 ; finds at, 78 ; age of, 85 ; excavations at, 88
Zimbaoe, 59, 96
Zinc, 103
Zodiac, 93

THE END